REVISE FOR

EDEXCEL

MODULAR science

Graham Booth
Bob McDuell
John Parker

Heinemann

Foundation

Heinemann Educational Publishers
Halley Court, Jordan Hill, Oxford, OX2 8EJ
a division of Reed Educational & Professional Publishing Ltd

Heinemann is a registered trademark of Reed Educational & Professional Publishing Ltd.

OXFORD MELBOURNE AUCKLAND JOHANNESBURG
BLANTYRE GABORONE IBADAN PORTSMOUTH (NH) CHICAGO

First published 2002

ISBN 0 435 578901

06 05 04 03 02
10 9 8 7 6 5 4 3 2 1

Edited by Sara Hulse

Index by Paul Nash

Typeset and illustrated by Tech Set Ltd

Printed and bound in Spain by Edelvives

Acknowledgements
Cover photo by Digitalvision
Photos by PhotoDisk

The publishers have made every effort to trace the copyright holders, but if they have inadvertently overlooked any, they will be pleased to make the necessary arrangements at the first opportunity.

Contents

Introduction

We have written this book to help you prepare in the best way possible for your exams.

Throughout the two years of your course you will sit a total of 12 module tests and two terminal exam papers. You can find tips on preparing for these in the *Examiners Tips* section (pages 146–152).

Make sure you find out the dates for your tests and exams to give yourself plenty of time to get ready for them.

Work through the chapter for the module you are about to sit. Pace yourself – do one spread at a time and look through your notes made in class.

↓

Try the questions at the end of every spread to check you really understand the topic.

↓

Check your answers under *Answers to end of spread questions*. Go back over anything you found difficult.

↓

Try the practice module questions at the end of each module. these are similar to your module test questions. Try to do them in the time allowed.

↓

Check your answers in the Answers to exam style questions at the end of the book.

↓

When you come to prepare for the terminal exams, look through all your notes and try the Exam style questions in this book.

Most importantly, Good luck!

The Authors

The human body – action and control

This module explains some of the most important life processes that take place in the human body, including digestion, control, excretion and defence.

The first topic in the module explains how the digestive system breaks down food to produce soluble nutrients suitable for absorption into the bloodstream.

A control system allows body activities to run smoothly. This is known as the nervous system and is covered in the second topic.

Topic three outlines the excretory functions of the kidneys and the final topic describes the structure and functions of the blood and the skin and explains their transport and defence functions.

The digestive system

You need to know

- ✔ the functions of the various parts of the digestive system;
- ✔ the principles of how enzymes work;
- ✔ the functions of a range of enzymes;
- ✔ how the products of digestion are absorbed into the bloodstream.

The process of digestion

A meal is full of useful nutrients but the food needs to be broken down into small, soluble molecules that can pass into the bloodstream. The process of breaking food down happens in stages and is called **digestion**.

Food is broken down by digestive juices, which contain the substances responsible for this breakdown – known as **enzymes**.

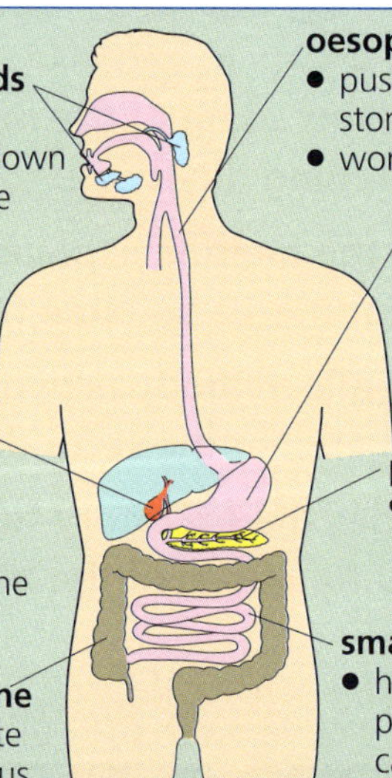

The human digestive system

The action of enzymes

Enzymes are sometimes called **biological catalysts**. An enzyme is a substance that:

- speeds up a chemical reaction;
- allows a chemical of a suitable shape to 'fit in';
- results in new substance(s) being formed;
- is unchanged at the end of a reaction, ready to be used again;
- works best at an **optimum temperature** (37°C);
- works best at an **optimum pH**.

Remember that you will be examined on the function of the parts of the digestive system (not the names or their position!).

Above this temperature reactions are slower. If the temperature is too high, enzymes are destroyed or **denatured**. Below 37°C reactions also slow down and if the temperature is too low the enzymes remain **inactive**.

The **optimum conditions** for enzyme-catalysed reactions involve the interaction of the following factors: temperature, pH, amount of substrate, amount of enzyme.

Each enzyme has a special shape. A substance of the correct shape can fit into the enzyme and be broken down into smaller molecules. Only then will a reaction take place.

Enzyme	Produced by...	Acts on...	Takes place in...	To produce...
carbohydrase	salivary gland	starch	mouth	sugar
protease	gastric gland	protein	stomach	chains of amino acids
carbohydrase	pancreas	starch	small intestine	sugar
lipase	pancreas	fats and oils	small intestine	fatty acid and glycerol

The function of bile in digestion

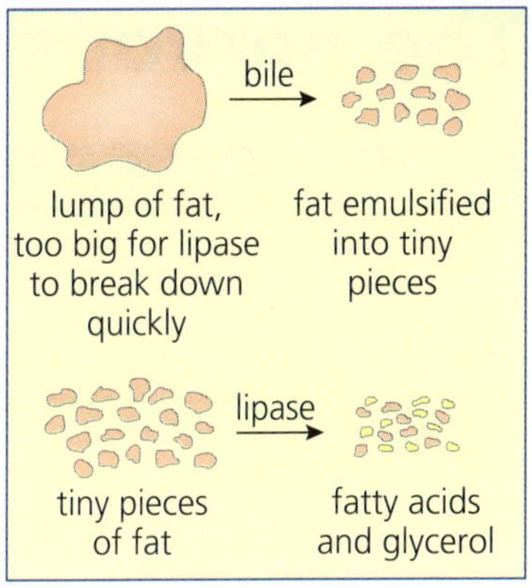

Bile helps digestion because:

- It breaks up fats and oil into tiny pieces, giving them a large surface area. This allows lipase to change them into fatty acids and glycerol more efficiently.
- Bile is an alkali. It neutralises the acid from the stomach as it passes into the small intestine, allowing the enzymes in the small intestine to work at a suitable pH.

Absorption of nutrients

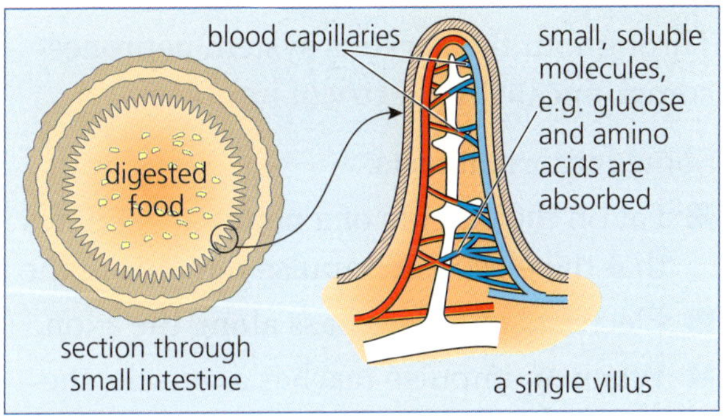

When the food reaches the small intestine, it has been broken down into molecules small enough to be absorbed into the bloodstream.

Special features of the small intestine help in the efficient absorption of nutrients:

- The small intestine is very long, and has large numbers of villi, giving it a large surface area through which nutrients can be absorbed.
- Each villus has the special function of absorption. The lining of the villas is only one cell thick so that nutrients can easily pass into the blood capillaries.

Nutrients pass through the wall of each villus into the blood. The nutrient molecules move from where they are in high concentration to where they are in low concentration. This is called **diffusion**.

Each of the villi is known as a villus. There are millions of them, so huge amounts of nutrients can be absorbed.

What happens in the large intestine?

By the time food reaches the large intestine many nutrients have been absorbed. Some undigested food arrives and continues to pass through the large intestine.
Water is absorbed into the bloodstream, which makes this waste more solid. This waste is known as faeces and passes from the body through the anus.

Questions

1. What conditions allow an enzyme to work at its fastest rate?
2. What happens to an enzyme at a very high temperature?
3. What happens to an enzyme at a very low temperature?
4. What happens to protein in the mouth? Give a reason for your answer.
5. Describe two features of the small intestine that give a high surface area for the absorption of nutrients.

The nervous system

You need to know

- the structure and function of a nerve cell;
- the functions of key parts of the eye;
- some effects of a range of drugs on the nervous system.

The nerve cells

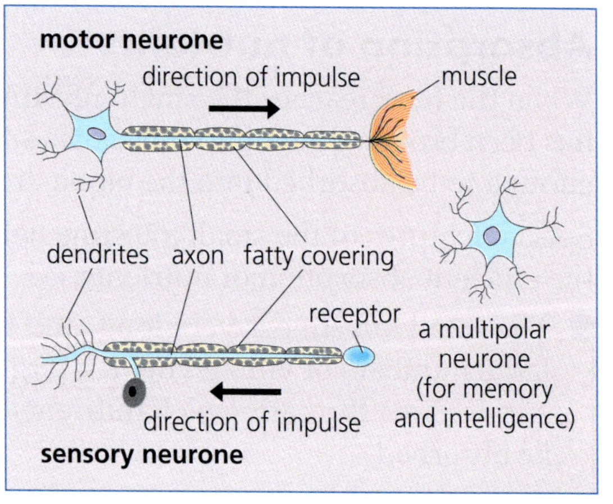

Each nerve cell is known as a **neurone**. Throughout the nervous system neurones communicate by **electrical impulses**.

Some important facts:

- Fat on the outside of a neurone insulates it so that the electrical impulse remains in the cell.
- Electrical impulses pass along the axon.
- When an impulse reaches a muscle, the muscle contracts.
- A receptor is found only on a sensory cell. A receptor responds to a stimulus such as light or temperature and sends an impulse back to the central nervous system.
- Sensory neurones supply information about the environment inside and outside the body. As a result of this other neurones respond.

The eye

The eye is one of the most important sensory organs in the body.

The iris reflex

The amount of light that enters the eye has to be controlled:

- too much light and the retina is damaged;
- too little light and you are unable to see.

Light reaches the retina at the back of the eye. An automatic reaction (a **reflex action**) takes place.

- Reflexes are very fast, because the impulse does not go to the brain.
- The muscles of the iris cause the pupil size to change.
- A wide pupil (**dilated**) allows more light to enter the eye.
- A narrow pupil (**constricted**) reduces the amount of light entering the eye.

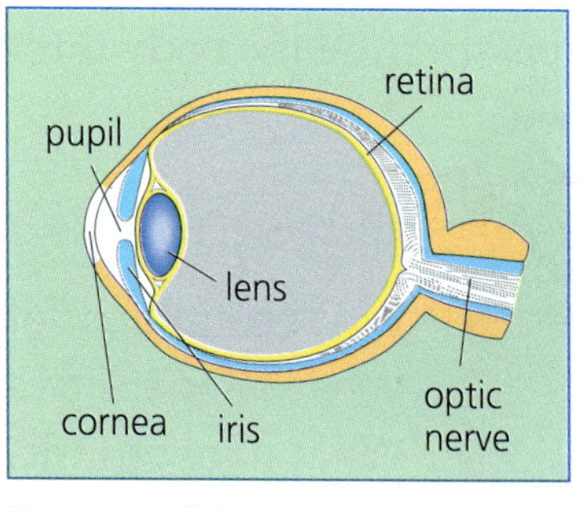

Structure of the eye

What is the function of the retina?

When we look at something, we focus its image on the **retina**, a layer at the back of the eye. Some neurones (**rods**) of the retina detect black and white, and some (**cones**) detect colour.

Electrical impulses travel from the retina through the optic nerve to the brain. When these impulses are received we can see.

The effects of drugs on the nervous system

Many substances have an effect on the body. Some drugs can be used to help relieve symptoms when people are ill. Some drugs can be misused and harm human health.

Drug	Problem
paracetamol – a painkiller	overdose damages the liver, and can cause death
heroin – a painkiller that can be given in a refined form known as morphine for serious conditions, especially terminal illness	very addictive
caffeine – found in coffee, this speeds up body reactions and so is known as a stimulant – it makes people more active	speeds up the heart rate
barbiturates – slow down reactions and are known as sedatives – make people less active – used as sleeping tablets	can be addictive
alcohol – a sedative, slowing down reactions	reaction times are slower, hence the dangers of drink-driving; destroys brain cells with regular use and can damage the liver
solvents – affect the working of the body in a number of ways, all bad	destroy nerve cells (neurones) and destroy the lungs, e.g. alveoli are badly damaged
tobacco – has an effect on the nerve cells but no useful function	addictive, increases risk of cancer, causes respiratory disease, e.g. bronchitis, and heart disease

Drugs can change behaviour and personality. Many crimes are drug-related and violence is a regular outcome. People have a lower resistance to viral infection.

Questions

1. How can white blood cells help to defend the body from harmful bacteria?
2. What are the functions of a blood clot?
3. Why is it important that light entering the eye is controlled?
4. What type of drug is alcohol? Give one problem that can result if someone drinks too much alcohol over a number of years.

The kidneys

You need to know

- why conditions in the body need to be kept constant, e.g. temperature, the amount of water;
- about the structure and function of the urinary system.

Homeostasis

Homeostasis is about the balance of body processes.

Processes in the body must be regulated. Too much of a chemical in the body leads to an imbalance, which can cause problems. Not enough of a chemical also results in imbalance. The amount needs to be just right. This is called **homeostasis** – keeping a constant internal environment.

If the body temperature is too high or too low then body processes become less efficient and we feel ill.

Your kidneys control the amount of water in your body. Every 5 minutes all the blood in your body passes through your kidneys. As the blood passes through excess water is removed. If your body is going to keep working, the amount of water inside must stay about the same. Your kidneys use the excess water to make urine which is stored in your bladder.

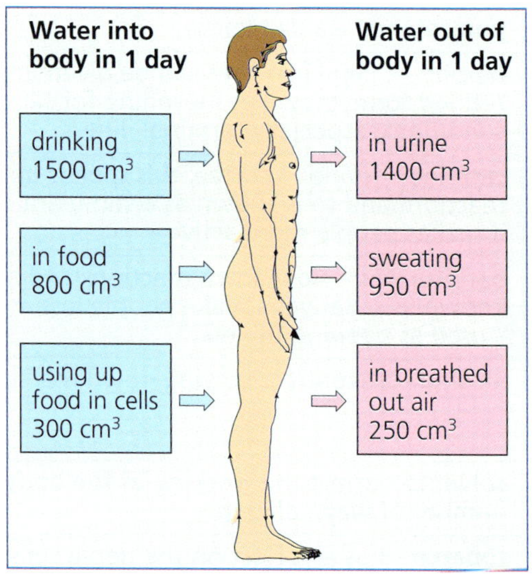

The amount of water taken in during the day, must equal the amount of water lost. In this diagram 2500 cm^3 of water enters the body and 2500 cm^3 is lost. Imagine what would happen if your body kept taking in more water than it lost!

The kidneys – the body's filter system

The kidneys are part of the urinary system:

- blood enters a kidney by the renal artery;
- the kidney filters out urea;
- urea and water move through the ureter to the bladder, forming urine;
- the filtered blood leaves by the renal vein;
- urine leaves the bladder by the urethra.

Students often mix up the kidneys and the liver. Remember that the liver makes the urea and the kidneys get rid of it!

Urea – a toxic substance

We eat food that contains proteins. After digestion, the proteins become amino acids, which enter the bloodstream. Amino acids are needed to build human protein, but can be dangerous if they reach high concentrations in the blood.

The liver converts excess amino acids into a less toxic substance – urea. Even urea is toxic, so must not be allowed to build up in the blood. The kidneys filter it out of the blood, and it is excreted in the urine.

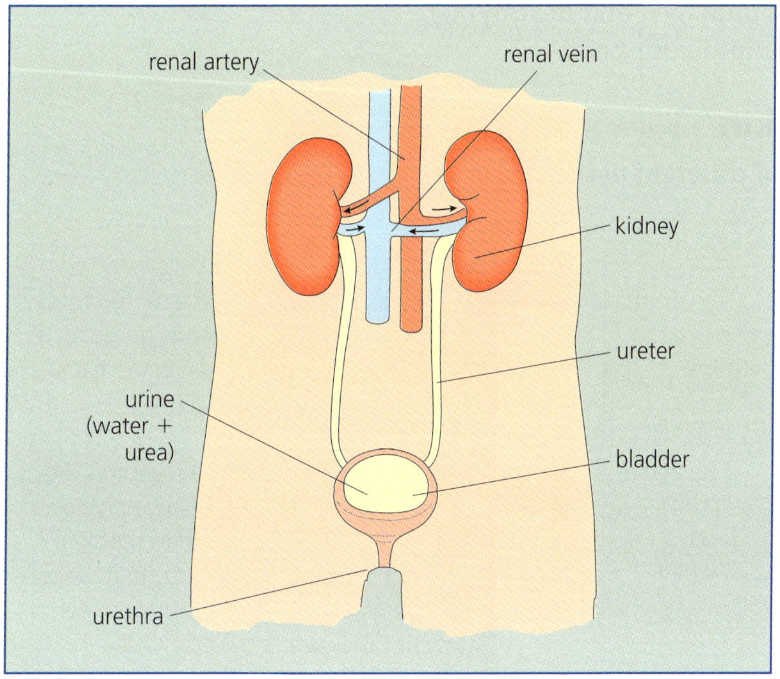

The human urinary system

Learn the terms ureter and urethra carefully. Many exam candidates mix them up – make sure that you don't!

Questions

1 Define homeostasis.
2 Which organ of the body makes urea?
3 Which organs of the body filter urea from the blood?
4 Name the tube that takes urea to the bladder.

Defence and protection

You need to know

- the structure of the skin;
- how the skin helps to control body temperature;
- how the skin helps to defend against infection;
- how the skin acts as a sense organ.
- the components of blood and their functions;
- the role of blood in transport around the body;
- about the clotting of blood.

Your skin is very important in preventing microorganisms entering your body. Your blood pays an important role in repairing skin when it becomes damaged and destroying any microorganisms that do get into your body.

The structure of the skin

The skin consists of a number of different tissues, each having a different function.

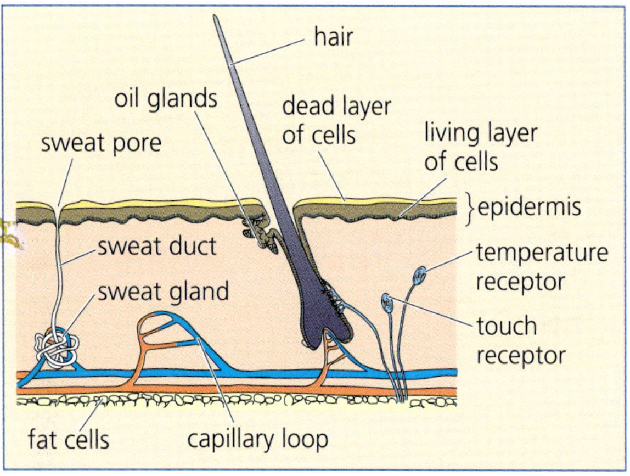

The structure of the skin

An outside layer of dead cells forms a tough barrier to prevent microorganisms entering the body. Oil glands produce sebum, which both lubricates the hairs and kills some microorganisms.

Touch receptors and nerve receptors are situated at the ends of sensory nerve cells. These receptors, embedded in the skin, send impulses to the brain, so that we can feel things that we touch, and can feel how hot they are.

The components of blood

The different components of blood include plasma, red blood cells, white blood cells and platelets (see diagram).

Plasma	White blood cells	Red blood cells
the liquid part of the blood	destroy microorganisms that invade the body	do not have a nucleus
carries the blood cells	are found as two different types	have a biconcave shape (like a doughnut)
carries all hormones		contain haemoglobin
carries nutrients such as glucose		transport oxygen
carries waste substances such as urea		

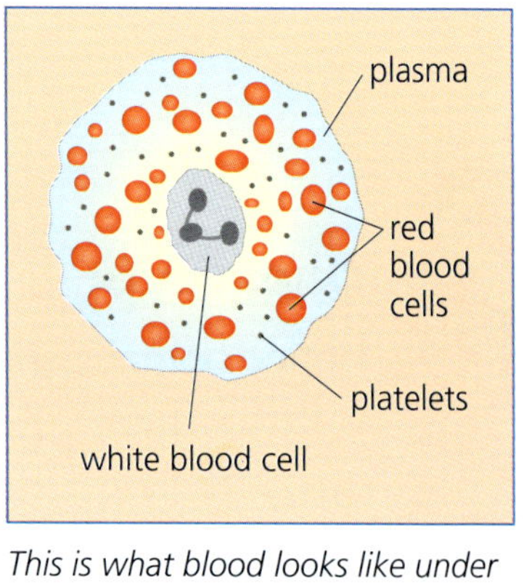

This is what blood looks like under a microscope

Blood clotting

Under normal body conditions blood flows along the vessels. When a vessel is damaged, the blood seems to change from a liquid to a solid, forming a clot. This stops blood flow in the vessel.

A blood clot is needed for two reasons:

- to prevent the loss of blood from a damaged vessel;
- to prevent the entry of microorganisms into the bloodstream.

The platelets produce fibres made of fibrin. These fibres form a mesh and trap the red blood cells, like fish in a net. This helps to form a scab.

White blood cells can destroy microorganisms

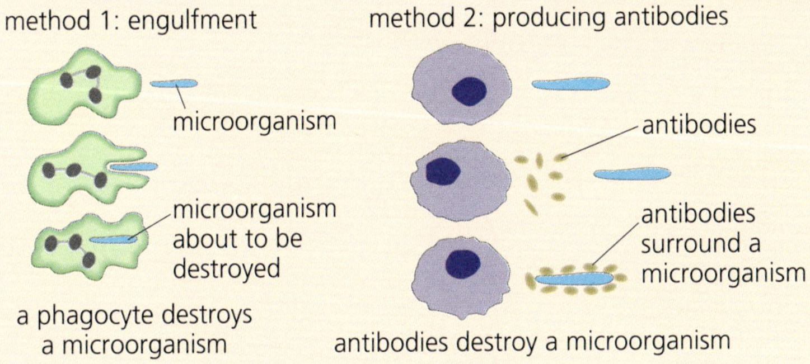

Control of body temperature

Sweat glands produce sweat, which flows onto the surface of the skin and evaporates. Evaporation needs heat energy, which is removed from the skin and so the body cools down.

The role of the skin capillaries:

- capillaries in the skin can be empty or full of blood;
- in warm conditions blood flows into them so that more heat can be lost to the air;
- in cold conditions blood flows out of them to deeper vessels in the body, so that less heat can be lost to the air.

If the body is too cold, the muscles make us shiver – this allows us to warm up again.

Body temperature is important for the functioning of enzymes. Enzymes do not work efficiently if the temperature is too high or too low.

Questions

1 Explain how a red blood cell is adapted for transporting oxygen efficiently.

2 How does sweating help to cool down the body?

Practice module test

You will have 17 minutes to answer these questions

1 The stomach digests:

- **A** starch
- **B** sugar
- **C** fat
- **D** protein

2 Enzymes in humans work best at:

- **A** very high temperatures
- **B** low temperatures
- **C** at freezing point
- **D** at optimum temperature

3 Which of the following parts of the blood can kill harmful microorganisms?

- **A** red blood cells
- **B** white blood cells
- **C** platelets
- **D** plasma

4 How does a blood clot prevent blood loss?

- **A** the fibres produce platelets
- **B** red blood cells are trapped by fibres
- **C** white blood cells are trapped by fibres
- **D** plasma becomes very cold

5 Electrical impulses are carried by:

- **A** blood cells
- **B** blood plasma
- **C** neurones
- **D** kidney nephrons

6 Which part of the digestive system absorbs glucose?

- **A** large intestine
- **B** small intestine
- **C** stomach
- **D** pancreas

7 Which one of the following drugs slows down reaction times?

- **A** caffeine
- **B** sedatives
- **C** stimulants
- **D** antibiotics

8 Which of the following is the most sensitive part of the eye?

- **A** optic nerve
- **B** retina
- **C** cornea
- **D** iris

9 Urea enters the kidney by the:

- **A** renal artery
- **B** renal vein
- **C** ureter
- **D** urethra

10 The graph below shows small changes in body temperature over a 12-hour period. Which statement describes how the body temperature varies over this period?

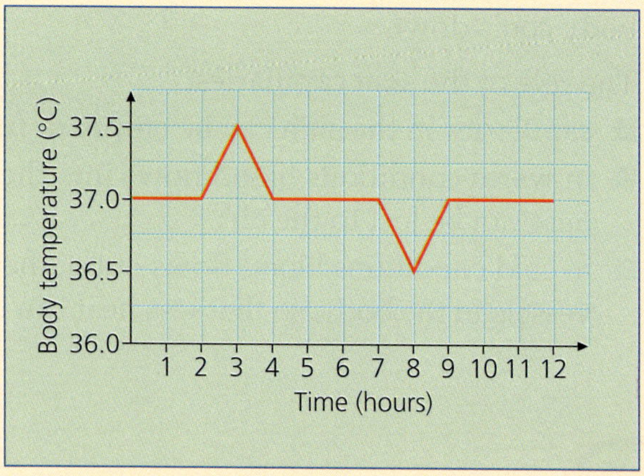

- **A** the temperature varies by ±1°C
- **B** the temperature varies by ±0.5°C
- **C** the temperature does not vary
- **D** the temperature varies by ±2°C

11 Which of the following structures provide a high surface area for the absorption of nutrients into the blood?

A villi
B salivary glands
C gall bladder
D pancreas

12 Saliva contains the enzyme:

A protease
B carbohydrase
C lipase
D maltase

13 Which of the following statements is not true:

A plasma helps the blood to clot
B the kidneys produce urea
C the large intestine absorbs water
D phagocytes engulf bacteria

14 Which of the following drugs speed up nervous impulses?

A stimulants
B painkillers
C hallucinogens
D sedatives

15 The following statements describe the process of sweating but they are in the wrong order:

1 water in sweat evaporates
2 the body cools down
3 the sweat glands produce sweat
4 sweat lies on the surface of the skin

Which of the following gives the correct order?

A 2 1 4 3
B 4 1 3 2
C 3 4 1 2
D 3 4 2 1

16 The graph below shows an enzyme-catalysed reaction.

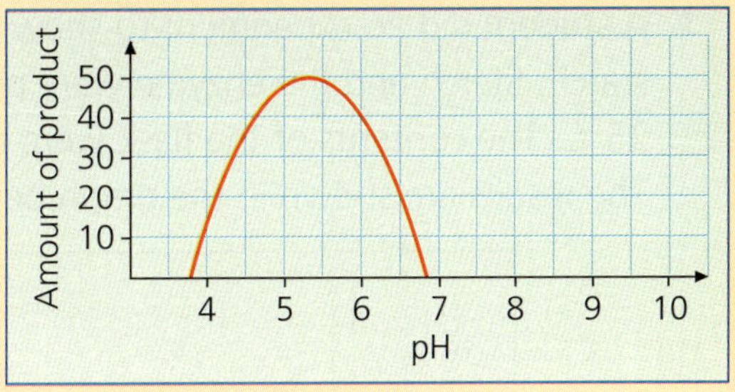

Which pH values would result in 40 arbitrary units of product?

A 4.8
B 6.4
C 4.8 and 6.4
D 5.5

17 Which of the following is **not** true of a red blood cell?

A it contains haemoglobin
B it is circular, so that it can pass through blood capillaries easily
C it has a nucleus
D it does not have a nucleus

18 Hormones are transported to the target organ:

A in the blood plasma
B by red blood cells
C by white blood cells
D by platelets

19 Paracetamol is a painkiller. It can be dangerous because:

A it is addictive
B it can harm the liver if taken in overdose
C it reduces reaction time
D it causes hallucinations

20 The enzyme lipase breaks down fats into:

A amino acids
B fatty acid and glycerol
C amino acids and glycerol
D sugars

Answers to these questions can be found on pages 140–144

Getting it right

1 A student did an experiment to show the effect of enzyme X on starch. Starch and the enzyme were put into a flask and kept at 25°C. The contents of the flask were measured every 10 minutes. The results are shown in the graph below.

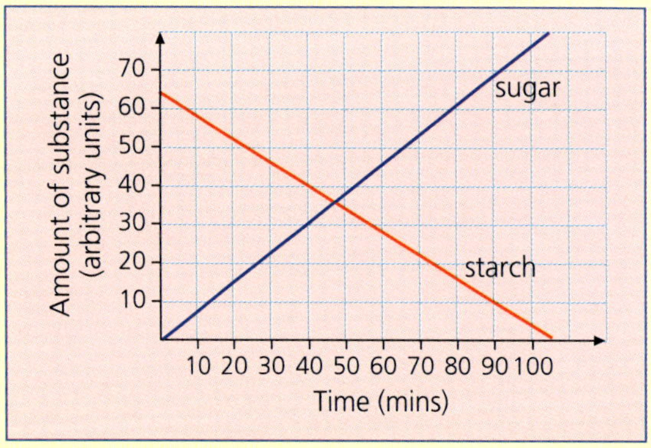

This graph gives you a good tip for exams! The fall in amount of one substance is often linked to a rise in another.

(a) (i) How much starch was there in the flask at the start of the experiment?

64 (arbitrary) units **[1]**

arbitrary units are units that represent any units.

(ii) After how many minutes was the amount of starch equal to the amount of sugar?

47 **[1]**

Always look carefully at where graph lines cross. Here the intersection gives you the answer.

(b) Describe and explain the changes in the amounts of each substance shown in the graph.

Starch – the amount of starch decreased during the experiment. Enzyme X broke down the starch. Sugar – the amount of sugar increased during the experiment. As starch broke down it formed sugar.

[4]

(c) Name enzyme X.

Carbohydrase **[1]**

Amylase is an example of a carbohydrase.

(d) What effect would a temperature of 37°C have if the experiment was repeated?

Sugar would be produced more quickly **[1]**

Did you remember that 37°C is the optimum (best) temperature for enzymes in humans?

Inheritance and survival

Genes control the characteristics of living things and have a major influence on survival. This module is about genes, the mechanism of inheritance and the effect of the environment on the expression of genes.

The first topic in the module is about human chromosomes and how characteristics are passed on through sexual reproduction.

The role of DNA in variation and inheritance is the subject of the second topic. This leads to topic three, which includes an outline of gene modification and the reasons for its use.

Species have changed over millions of years. The fourth topic explores aspects of natural selection and survival that have led to the evolution of different species.

Humans can harm their own existence and that of other living things by polluting the environment. The effects of pollution are explored in this final topic.

Chromosomes and variation

You need to know

- the numbers of chromosomes in human body cells and sex cells;
- that sex is controlled by specialised chromosomes – the X and Y chromosomes;
- the role of human sex cells in fertilisation;
- how sexual reproduction results in variation across the human population;
- the functions of male and female sex hormones.

Human body cells

A human adult consists of around 5 billion cells. Different cells do different jobs but there is one common structure in every cell – the **nucleus**. The human nucleus contains 23 pairs of **chromosomes**, known as the **diploid number**. Each chromosome is like a row of **genes**, each of which controls a particular human characteristic.

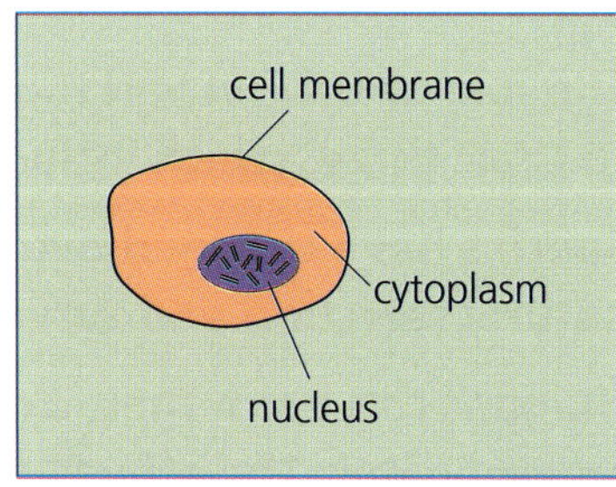

Human sex cells

Sex cells are produced by both men and women and carry the chromosomes responsible for male and female characteristics. There are two different sex chromosomes in the nucleus – X and Y. A male has an X and a Y chromosome. A female has two X chromosomes. Each sex cell carries 23 single chromosomes (22 + X or 22 + Y). This single set of 23 chromosomes is called the **haploid number**.

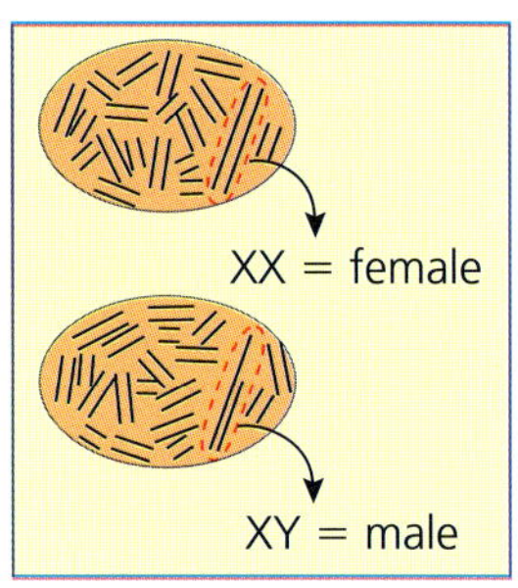

An X chromosome is longer than a Y chromosome. This means there are more genes on one side (X) than on the other (Y).

Remember – only one sperm "wins" and fuses with an egg.

Fertilisation

This is the fusion of the male sex cell (**sperm**) with the female egg cell (**ovum**) to form one cell, a fertilised egg cell or **zygote**. Males produce sperm that carry *either* 22 single chromosomes plus X *or* 22 single chromosomes plus Y. Females can only produce eggs that carry 22 single chromosomes plus X. The sex of a baby depends only on whether the sperm that reaches the egg first carries X or Y.

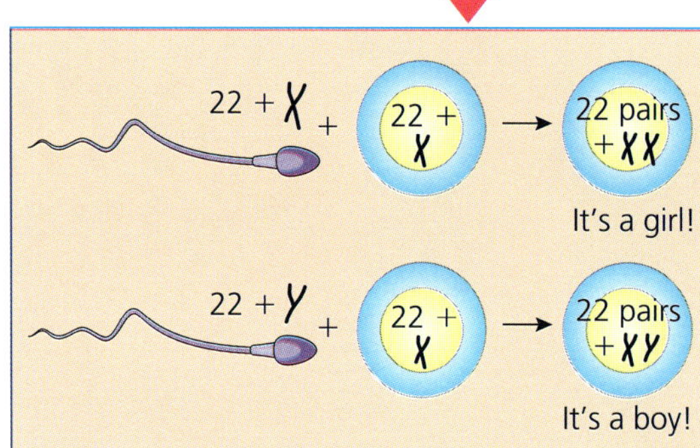

Sexual reproduction and variation

A man may produce 200 million sperm in one ejaculation. Each sperm produced is different to the next. Every egg produced by a woman is different. This is why children look noticeably different to their parents – this is known as **variation**.

Both parents pass on genes to a baby. A gene may be a feature such as eye colour. We all know that there are different eye colours (blue, brown, grey, etc.). Each colour is a different expression of the same gene, known as an **allele**. For each feature of a baby, one allele is inherited from the mother and one from the father. Each allele can be either **dominant** or **recessive**.

The sex hormones

Hormones are produced by endocrine glands. Each hormone is like a chemical message that is transported through the body in the blood. The sex hormones are very important in giving a person the characteristic features of their sex – for example the deep voice of a teenage boy or the enlargement of breasts in a teenage girl.

Girls produce sex hormones at an earlier age than boys – they mature first.

These hormones cause the **secondary sexual characteristics** to develop – the changes that take place during the teenage years.

Name of hormone	Where is the hormone produced?	How does it reach its target?	What effect does it have?
testosterone	testes	in blood	• deep voice • sperm production • wide shoulders • pubic hair • facial hair
oestrogen	ovaries	in blood	• egg production • hips become wider • breasts become bigger • pubic hair • lining of uterus builds up during menstrual cycle
progesterone	ovaries	in blood	keeps the lining of the uterus in place needed during pregnancy

Questions

1 What is the function of **a** oestrogen **b** progesterone?

2 What is fertilisation?

Genes and variation

You need to know

- about DNA as a unit of inheritance;
- the mechanism of monohybrid inheritance;
- that the environment can affect inherited characteristics;
- that some diseases can be inherited;
- some implications of the Human Genome Project;
- the causes and consequences of changes in DNA (mutation);
- that DNA can be artificially changed by gene modification.

DNA – the secret of life!

Genes control human characteristics and are made from **D**eoxyribo**N**ucleic **A**cid – DNA. DNA consists of:

- two strands, twisted to form a double helix;
- strands that are linked together like the rungs of a ladder;
- the links are made by **bases** that join together in specific pairs – **thymine** (T) links to **adenine** (A) and **cytosine** (C) links to **guanine** (G);

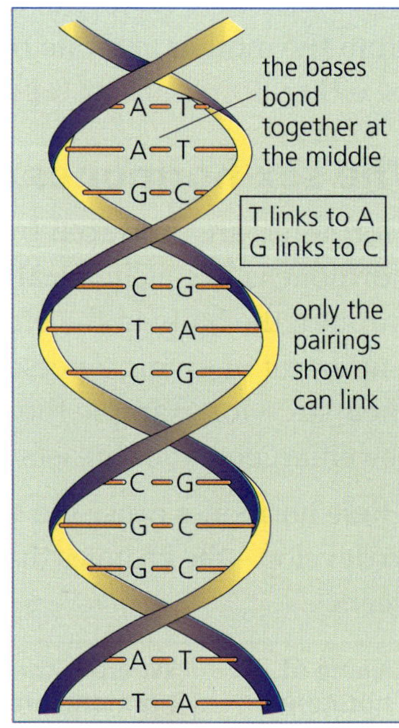

DNA is a very long molecule – the more genes along DNA, the longer it is. Chromosomes are different lengths because some have more genes than others.

Changes in DNA

Changes in DNA are called **mutations**. A gene may change into a new form, e.g. an allele for white petals may change to one producing red petals. An extra chromosome may even appear, or extra genes may be added or deleted.

Changes in DNA can be caused by:

- radiation (X-rays and gamma rays);
- ultraviolet light;
- substances produced when tobacco is burned.

Monohybrid inheritance

Two organisms may show a difference, e.g. eye colour.
Allele for brown eyes = B (dominant)
Allele for blue eyes = b (recessive)
Monohybrid inheritance follows the pattern shown below.

Monohybrid inheritance follows the pattern shown below.

parent BB → sex cells (B) (B) × parent bb → sex cells (b) (b)

children:

	B	B
b	Bb	Bb
b	Bb	Bb

Bb is a hybrid that carries blue.
100% of offspring have brown eyes.

Crossing two similar offspring, monohybrid inheritance continues with the following pattern.

parent Bb → sex cells (B) (b) × parent Bb → sex cells (B) (b)

children:

	B	b
B	BB	Bb
b	Bb	bb

BB = pure bred brown eyes.
Bb = hybrid has brown eyes carries blue.
bb = pure bred blue eyes.
Children are 75% brown and 25% blue OR 3:1 brown to blue.

Genetic diseases

Some genes can be faulty and cause a **genetic disease**, which can be inherited. The chances of inheriting a genetic disease are affected by whether the faulty allele is dominant or recessive, and on which chromosome the gene is located.

The Human Genome Project
- mapped the genes along the chromosomes
- may help to identify genes responsible for disease
- may result in cures being found

How does the environment affect genes?

Genes control the manufacture of proteins in the cells. Proteins are used to make structures. For example, the weight of a baby at birth depends on a number of factors:

- the genes of the developing fetus;
- the diet of its mother during her pregnancy;
- other substances that pass into the blood of the fetus during development, including drugs such as nicotine;
- the health of the mother.

Asexual reproduction

Some organisms can reproduce without using any sex cells. Parent cells divide to produce cells that are genetically identical to the parent. The new cells are **clones** of the parent. Examples include:

- Spider plants (Chlorophytum) – drooping stems hang towards the soil and develop roots. Mini-plants develop that root into the soil, forming clones of the parent plant.
- During their life cycle, female greenfly produce young without any fertilisation. Their cells simply divide to form the new generation.

Although both the spider plant and the greenfly reproduce asexually, sexual reproduction is also used, which produces offspring more quickly.

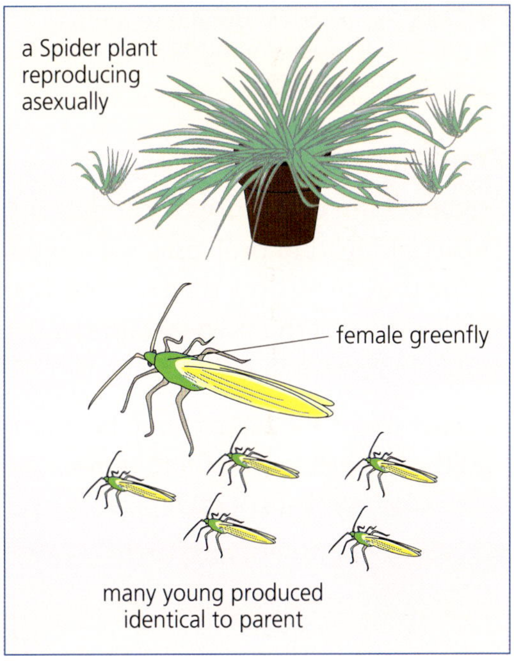

Questions

1 In a DNA molecule, which base links to (a) cytosine, (b) thymine?
2 Suggest one advantage of the Human Genome Project?
3 Define asexual reproduction.

Selection, survival and evolution

You need to know

- ✔ the ways in which organisms are adapted to their environment;
- ✔ factors that affect numbers in the populations of a variety of species;
- ✔ the principles of natural selection leading to evolution;
- ✔ the principles of selective breeding (artificial selection);
- ✔ about pollution and human survival.

How can adaptations help an organism to survive?

Organisms that successfully live in their habitat have **adaptations** that make them suited to their environment. The examples below illustrate typical adaptations.

Organisms in your exam questions may be different but they will display similar adaptations.

Arctic fox	Fennec fox
habitat – cold	Habitat – warm
• small ears to reduce surface area for heat loss • long fur, traps air, good insulation • white fur, good camouflage, not seen by predators or prey	• large ears to increase surface area for heat loss • short fur, not good insulation, easy to lose heat • brown fur, good camouflage, not seen by predators or prey

Predators and prey

Predators are **carnivores** – animals that eat other animals. This could lead to problems – if a predatory species kills all the prey in an area then it would cause its own death. The key part of the predator–prey relationship is that numbers remain in balance.

An example is the relationship between the lynx (predator) and the snowshoe hare (herbivorous prey). The graph below shows the numbers of each population from 1910 to 1970.

Take care when answering questions about animals that eat plants like cacti. They are not carnivores – they are herbivores!

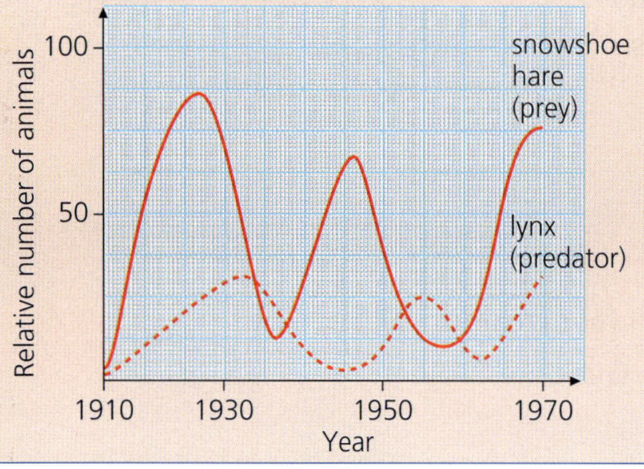

- each spring, plants grow so there is more food for the hares;
- the hare population breeds and numbers increase;
- predators have more hares to kill, so hare numbers decrease;
- the lynx (predator) population has a lot of food available and reproduces, so increasing in numbers;
- more lynx need more food, but there are now fewer hares, so their population decreases again;

Competition

This happens when organisms have the same needs. With a limited amount of food available, there is not enough for all organisms. Those better adapted to 'fight for their share' are good competitors. Others may perish.

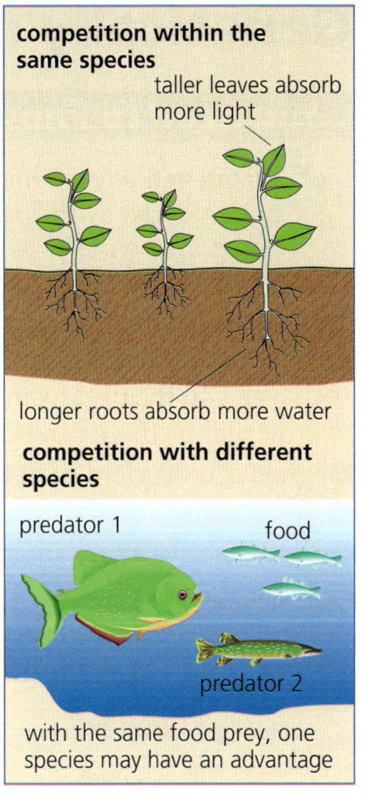

Natural selection

Natural selection was first proposed by Charles Darwin. He observed the differences across species throughout the world. The key part to understanding this theory is that within a species there is **genetic variation**:

- different alleles may give individuals a better adaptation to the environmental conditions;
- some individuals die;
- some individuals survive and go on to pass on their alleles to the next generation, which now have the genetic advantage.

Why do some members of a species have different adaptations?

1. Sexual reproduction produces different combinations of alleles.
2. New genes and alleles appear occasionally – these are **mutations**.

Mutations appear spontaneously. A mutation can be good or bad for the species. Some bad mutations resulted in the death of a species. This is **extinction**. Good mutations result in changes to species over the years. This is **evolution** – it continues to take place today.

Is there evidence that evolution has taken place?

Yes! Organisms died millions of years ago. Most rotted down completey but some did not. The remains can be found today and are known as **fossils**. Many fossils are so well preserved that we can find out accurate details of their structure.

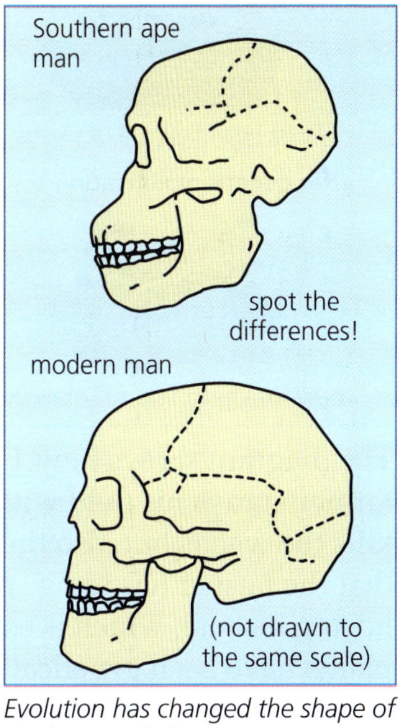

Evolution has changed the shape of the human skull

Questions

1. Explain the advantage of a genetic modifications which makes a crop plant resistant to weedkiller
2. What can cause an increase in the number of herbivores in an area?
3. Name two substances which plants compete for?

Genetically modified organisms

You need to know

- that genetically modified organisms are produced by the transfer of genes from a donor to a recipient;
- the benefits of genetic modification.

Transfer of a gene from one organism to another can be of great benefit. The technique can be used to give **disease resistance** to the organism receiving the gene. In the case of crop plants, there can be several advantages:

- greater crop yield than for conventional crops;
- resistance to attack by fungi;
- resistance to attack by insects;
- better rate of photosynthesis;
- crop products that lack allergy-causing chemicals, e.g. cereals may be made gluten-free.

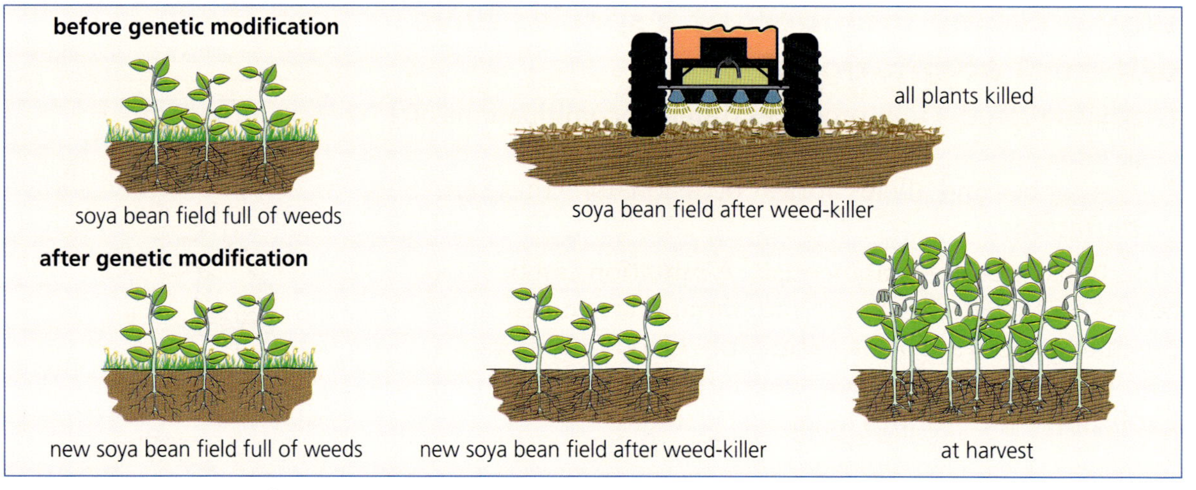

The diagram shows how, before genetic modification, the farmer sprays his field with weed-killer – this not only kills the weeds but also the soya bean plants. This means that the farmer has to use mechanical methods such as hoeing instead, which is expensive. After the soya bean plants have been genetically modified, they are resistant to the weed-killer, giving high crop yields with no weeds.

Questions

1 Explain why GM soya bean plants are resistant to weed-killer, but traditional soya bean plants are not.

2 Explain why GM soya bean plants give a higher yield of beans than the conventional crop.

Pollution (and human survival)

You need to know

- ✔ that human activities cause pollution?
- ✔ the causes and effects of acid rain.

A bigger human population has increased needs. More food, more buildings, more cars, more products from industry are required. The list seems endless.

These requirements result in substances and processes that are harmful to the environment – this is **pollution**. Humans are responsible!

You may be given data to analyse. Look out for population increases and data involving additional needs, resulting in pollution.

Acid rain

Acid rain is produced when:

- fossil fuels such as coal and petrol are burned;
- sulphur dioxide is released into the air;
- the sulphur dioxide combines with water vapour in the air;
- this forms sulphurous acid (acid rain).

Acid rain can corrode buildings, kill plants and destroy aquatic life – even complete food chains can be destroyed.

Larger human populations mean increased traffic – this can also lead to the formation of acid rain. Exhaust gases from vehicles contain other gases as well as sulphur dioxide – carbon monoxide, carbon dioxide and nitrogen oxides – these can also form acid rain. Pollution from car exhausts can be reduced by using a catalytic converter – this reduces the toxic emissions from car exhausts. Alternatively, we could use vehicles that do not give off toxic substances, e.g. electric or solar-powered vehicles.

Other pollutants – like smoke – can also cause problems. Dust particles in smoke can cover plants and reduce photosynthesis.

Questions

1. Coal-fired power stations in the UK produce sulphur dioxide fumes. How can they pollute countries such as Sweden?
2. Name three pollutants found in car exhaust fumes.

Practice module test

You will have 17 minutes to answer these questions

1 Which of these substances causes acid rain?

- **A** phosphate
- **B** sulphur dioxide
- **C** nitrogen
- **D** oxygen

2 Which of these would decrease the amount of carbon dioxide in the air?

- **A** cutting down trees
- **B** planting more trees
- **C** burning wood
- **D** burning fossil fuels

3 Genes are part of:

- **A** cell walls
- **B** cytoplasm
- **C** cell membranes
- **D** chromosomes

4 Which of the following hormones results in the shoulders of male teenagers becoming broader?

- **A** oestrogen
- **B** progesterone
- **C** testosterone
- **D** adrenaline

5 A gamete:

- **A** is a sex cell
- **B** carries both X and Y chromosomes
- **C** carries 23 pairs of chromosomes
- **D** is a body cell

6 Asexual reproduction:

- **A** does not produce clones
- **B** takes place with two sexes
- **C** produces cells that are genetically the same
- **D** produces cells that are genetically different

7 The diagram shows a cactus plant. One way in which a cactus is adapted to survive in desert conditions is:

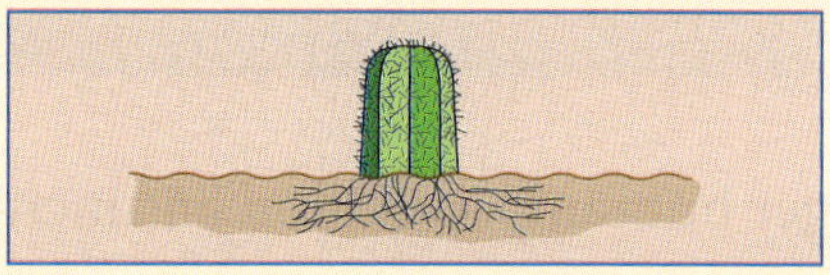

- **A** it has a large root network
- **B** it has a small root network
- **C** it loses a lot of water by evaporation
- **D** it has no waxy cuticle

8 A wheat plant with resistance to fungus is chosen to cross with a wheat plant of high yield. This is an example of:

- **A** genetic engineering
- **B** selective breeding
- **C** asexual reproduction
- **D** producing genetically modified organisms

9 The allele for brown eyes (B) is dominant to the allele for blue eyes (b). A child inherits an allele for brown eyes and an allele for blue eyes. What is the colour of the child's eyes?

- **A** blue
- **B** brown
- **C** grey
- **D** bluey-brown

10 The diagram below shows **one** change in the uterus. The female hormone that caused this change is:

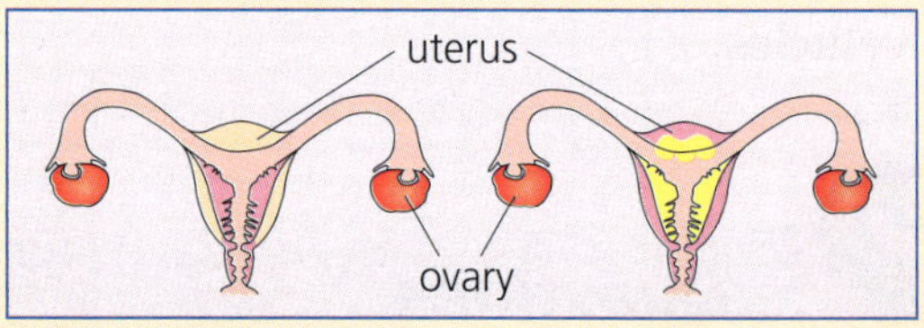

- **A** progesterone
- **B** testosterone
- **C** adrenaline
- **D** oestrogen

11 Given below is a sequence of bases in a DNA molecule. What are the missing bases?

A A T G C C
T T A ___ ___ ___

A = adenine, T = thymine,
G = guanine, C = cytosine

A T T A
B G G C
C C G G
D C C G

12 Evolution:

A takes place when a species becomes extinct
B no longer takes place
C consists of changes to species over millions of years
D does not rely on mutations to take place

13 Differences in the weight of people is caused by:

A just the environment
B just the genes
C genes plus the environment
D just food

14 Choose the correct line from the following table to show how fertilisation produces a baby boy.

	sperm	+	egg	=	fertilised egg
A	XX	+	XX	=	XXXX
B	X	+	Y	=	XY
C	X	+	X	=	XX
D	XY	+	Y	=	XXY

15 In a flower the allele for red petals (R) is dominant to the one for white petals (r). If plants of the genotypes rr and Rr are crossed, what would the next generation be?

A 50% red, 50% white
B 50% pink, 50% white
C 75% red, 25% white
D 25% red, 75% white

16 Ladybirds are predators of greenfly. The food of greenfly is the sap of plants. Ladybirds increase in numbers:

A before an increase in greenfly
B after an increase in greenfly
C when plants die down
D during the winter

17 Which of these can cause mutations in skin cells?

A sweating too much
B eating too much protein
C too much muscular activity
D ultraviolet light

18 A sperm cell carries the following number of chromosomes:

A 22
B 23
C 24
D 46

19 Acid rain is dangerous because:

A it makes the pH of lakes very high
B by destroying plants it destroys food chains
C it causes skin cancer
D it increases the mineral level in soil

20 During one year a lake became more acidic as a result of high rainfall. Which graph below (**A**, **B**, **C** or **D**) shows this?

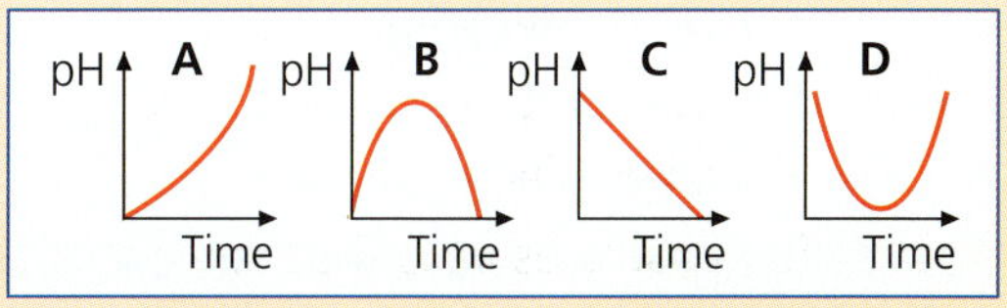

Answers to these questions can be found on pages 140–144

Getting it right

1 Cystic fibrosis is a disease carried by a recessive allele. Mr and Mrs Henderson both carry the allele for cystic fibrosis but do not suffer any symptoms.

(a) Complete the genetic diagram below to show the possible children that the Hendersons can produce. (N = normal healthy allele for mucus production. n = cystic fibrosis allele.)

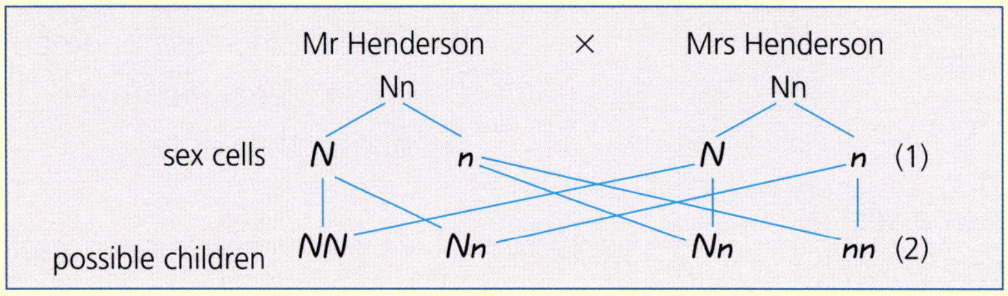

[3]

(b) What are the chances of the Hendersons having a baby with cystic fibrosis?

1 in 4 chance **[1]**

2 Complete the diagram below to show how the sex of a baby is determined.

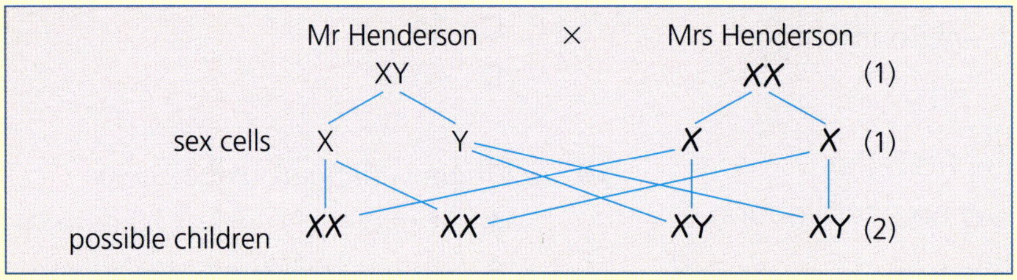

[4]

(b) What are the chances of the Hendersons having a baby boy?

1 in 2 chance **[1]**

(c) What are the chances of the Hendersons having a baby girl with cystic fibrosis?

1 in 8 chance **[1]**

Remember that an allele is an alternative from of a gene. N is a dominant allele.

Sex cells carry single sets of chromosomes.

The lines on the genetic diagram will help you follow the allele combination.

Remember that a male carries XY chromosomes and a female XX. The clues are given. If Mr Henderson is XY then Mrs Henderson must be XX.

The hardest part of the question is right at the end! If 1 in every 4 babies has cystic fibrosis, and half of them are females, then the chances of female sufferers is 1 in 8.

Chemical patterns

This module is about patterns that can be seen in:

- the arrangement of elements in the periodic table;
- the structure of atoms;
- the rates of chemical reactions;
- properties of the group of elements called halogens.

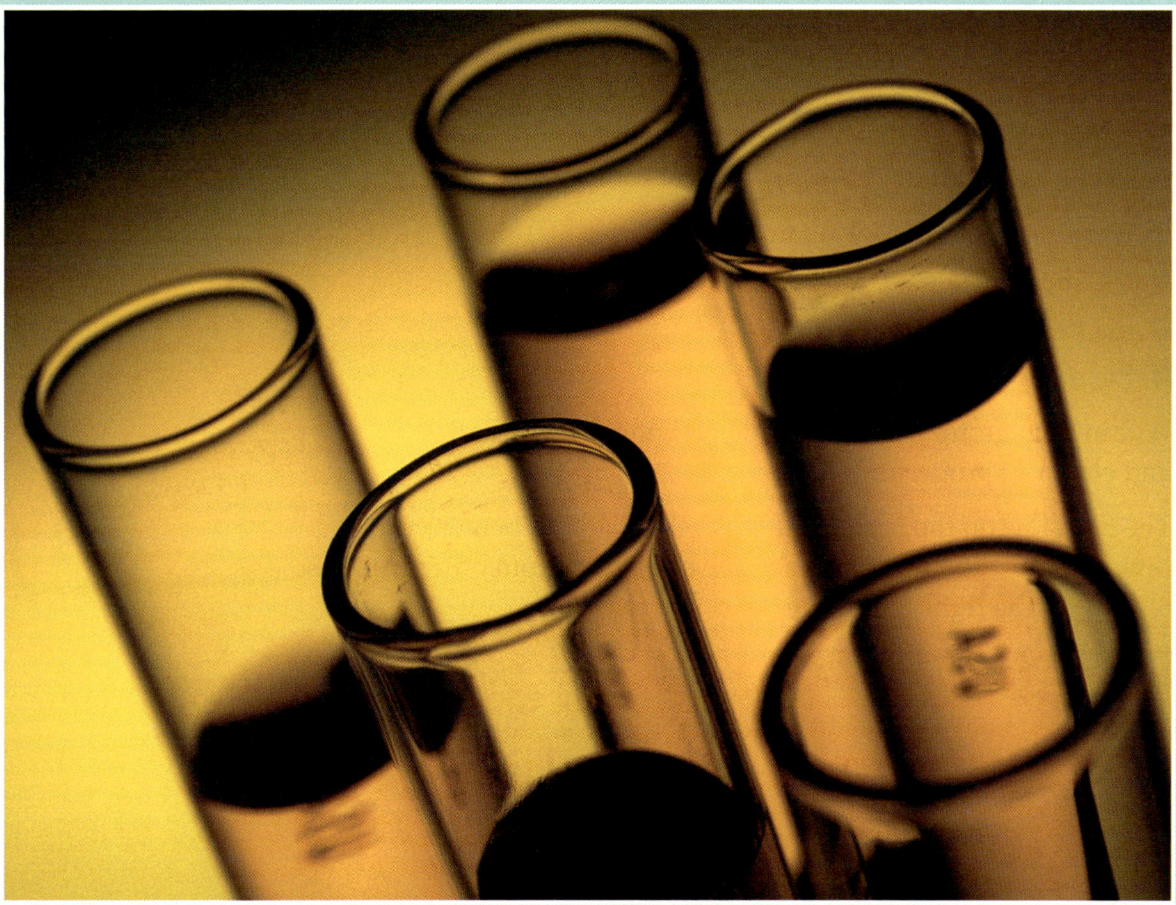

Elements and the periodic table

You need to know

- ✔ approximately 100 elements are arranged in order of increasing atomic number in the periodic table;
- ✔ metals are on the left-hand side of the periodic table and non-metals are on the right;
- ✔ elements in the same family have similar properties and are found in the same vertical column or group;
- ✔ examples of families are the alkali metals (Group 1), halogens (Group 7) and noble gases (Group 8);
- ✔ elements in the same group show a gradual change in properties from the top of the group to the bottom;
- ✔ there is a link between the arrangement of electrons around the nucleus of an atom of an element and its position in the periodic table;
- ✔ the number of electrons in the outer shell of an atom is the same as the group number of the element in the periodic table.

Structure of the periodic table

Elements are arranged in the **periodic table** in order of increasing **atomic number**. The horizontal rows of elements are called **periods**. Elements in the same family with similar properties are found in the same vertical column or **group**.

LI	F	He
Na	Cl	Ne
K	Br	Ar
Rb	I	Kr
Cs	At	Xe
Fr		Rn

Examples of three chemical families are:

- the alkali metals (in Group 1);
- the halogens (in Group 7);
- the noble gases (in Group 8).

Within each group there is a gradual change in physical and chemical properties.

A copy of the periodic table can be found on page 152.

The bold line on the periodic table in the diagram below divides **metals** on the left-hand side of the line from **non-metals** on the right-hand side.

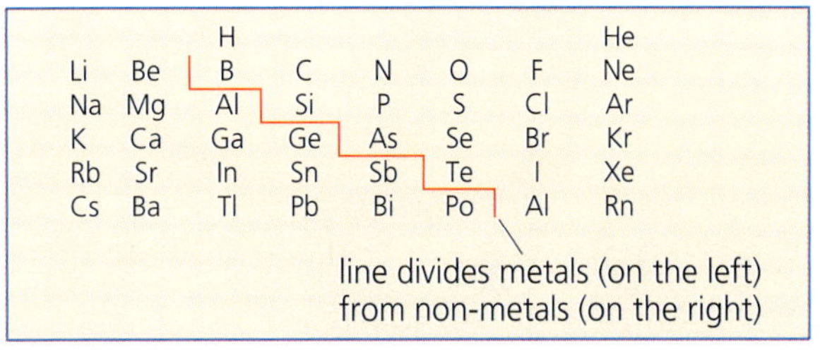

There is a pattern in the arrangement of electrons of the elements in the periodic table. The diagram on the next page shows the arrangement of electrons in atoms of the first 20 elements.

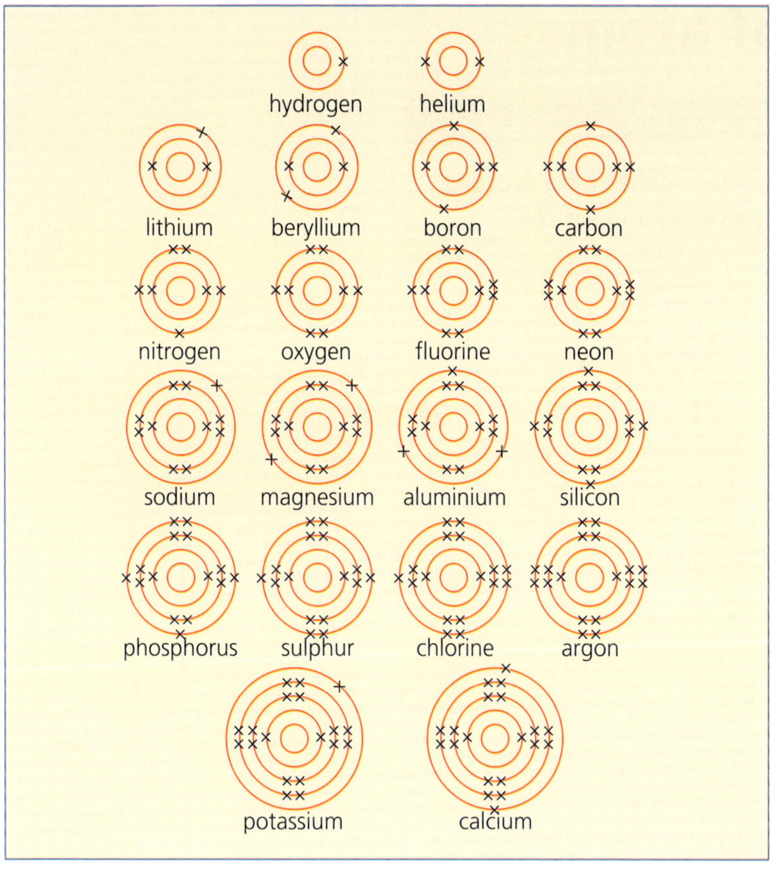

There is a pattern in the arrangement of electrons of the elements in the periodic table.

There is one exception – helium is in Group 8 but has two electrons in the outer shell.

The number of electrons in the outer shell of an atom of an element is the same as the group number of the element in the periodic table. For example, carbon is in Group 4 and so has four electrons in the outer shell.

Elements in a group of the periodic table have similar properties. The physical and chemical properties of the elements change gradually down a group.

This pattern in properties can be seen with the alkali metals in Group 1, noble gases in Group 8 and halogens in Group 7.

Questions

1. Look at the periodic table on page 152. Which element is in Period 3 and Group 5?
2. Is the element you found in Question 1 a metal or a non-metal?
3. Which of the elements below is in the same group as sodium?

   potassium   calcium   bromine   argon
4. How many electrons are there in the outer shell of a sulphur atom?

The structure of atoms

You need to know

✔ Atoms are made up from a nucleus containing protons and neutrons, with electrons moving around the nucleus in shells.

Particles in atoms

Three different types of particle make up all atoms – protons, neutrons and electrons. The table below gives information about these three particles.

Atoms are the smallest part of an element that can exist alone.

Particle	Mass	Charge
proton, p	1 unit	+1
neutron, n	1 unit	0
electron, e	negligible	−1

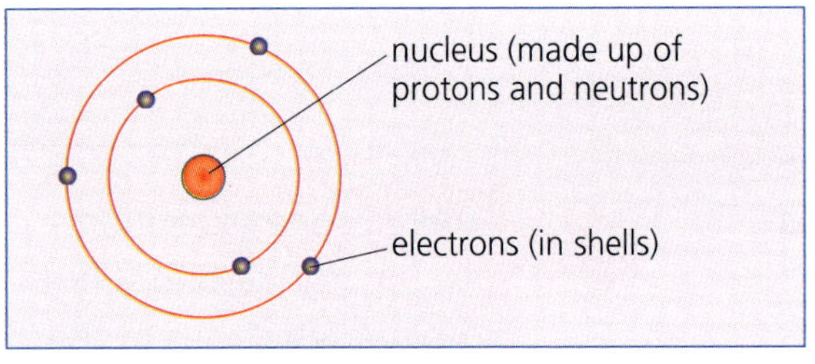

In atoms the protons and neutrons are in the **nucleus**. The protons and neutrons are tightly packed together. Electrons are arranged in shells around the nucleus. The nucleus of an atom is positively charged. Each atom has a **mass number** and an **atomic number**.

The atomic number is the number of protons in the nucleus of the atom.

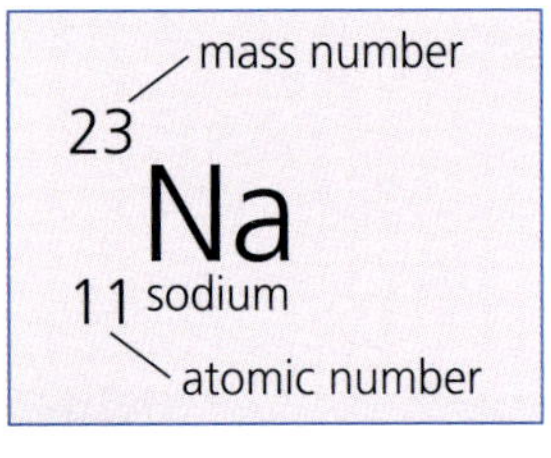

Questions

1 What are the two particles present in the nucleus of an atom?

2 Which particle has the smallest mass?

3 Which particle is not in the nucleus of an atom?

Rates of reaction

You need to know

✔ Different chemical reactions take place at different rates. The rate of a chemical reaction can be increased by:
- increasing temperature;
- increasing the concentration of a reactant;
- increasing the surface area of a reactant;
- using a catalyst.

Reactions take place when particles of the reactants collide. The rate of reaction is increased when there are more frequent collisions or when there is greater energy on the collisions.

Rates of reactions with enzymes vary with changes in temperature and pH.

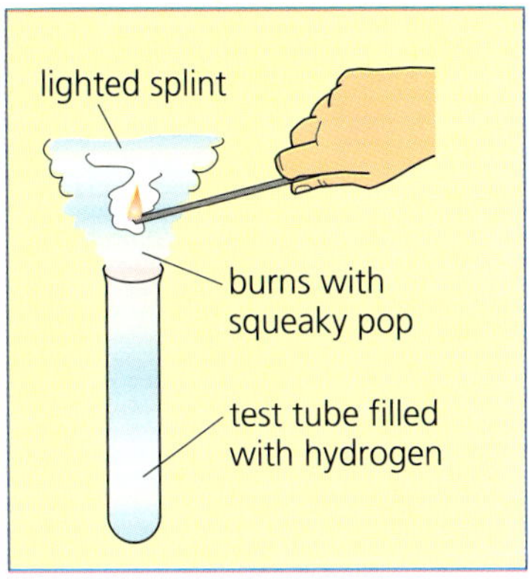

A very fast reaction

Chemical reactions take place at very different rates. For example, if a lighted splint is put into a test tube of hydrogen gas, the gas burns with a squeaky pop. This **explosion** is a very, very fast reaction and is finished in a tiny fraction of a second. This is a **very fast reaction**.

A limestone building will react with acidic gases in the atmosphere, but this reaction may take hundreds of years. This is a **very slow reaction**.

Remember that a fast reaction takes only a short time and a slow reaction takes a long time.

Effect of temperature on the rate of a reaction

Increasing temperature increases the rate of a reaction. For example, we know that milk turns sour more quickly when left outside the refrigerator, especially in summer. The reaction souring the milk goes faster at warmer temperatures.

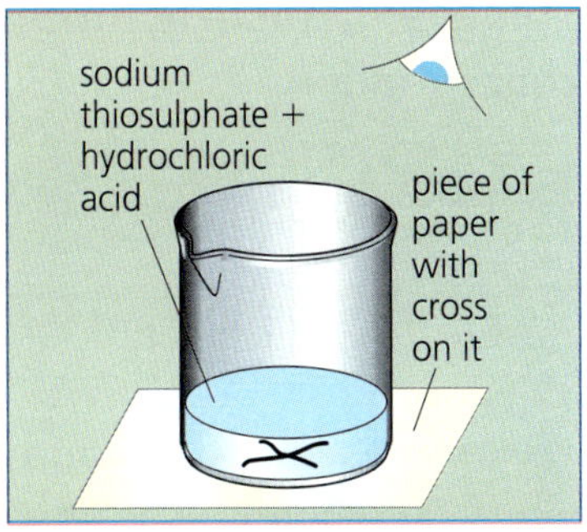

When solutions of sodium thiosulphate and dilute hydrochloric acid are mixed, a reaction takes place within a minute or so. One of the products is sulphur and this forms as a creamy precipitate. The reaction can take place in a beaker placed on a piece of paper with a cross on it. The solutions are mixed and the time taken for the cross to disappear from view is noted.

Temperature (°C)	Time taken for cross to disappear (s)
20	200
30	120
45	50
55	18

The equation for the reaction is:

sodium thiosulphate + hydrochloric acid → sodium chloride + sulphur dioxide + water + sulphur

If the same reaction is carried out but at different temperatures, it can be seen that as the temperature increases the time taken for the cross to disappear decreases.

continued ⟶

Effect of concentration on the rate of a reaction

Magnesium and dilute hydrochloric acid react together to produce magnesium chloride and hydrogen gas. Magnesium dissolves in the solution.

magnesium + hydrochloric acid → magnesium chloride + hydrogen

If the reaction is carried out using equal masses of magnesium but with different concentrations of dilute hydrochloric acid, a pattern can be seen in the results. As the concentration of dilute hydrochloric acid increases, the time taken for the magnesium to disappear decreases – the reaction gets faster.

Concentration (g/dm^3)	Time taken for magnesium to disappear (s)
10	65
20	48
25	38
30	30
40	18

Effect of particle size on the rate of a reaction

In coal mines, coal dust mixed with air can explode. There is no risk of coal exploding when it is in lumps – in fact you might have difficulty getting lumps of coal to burn. Calcium carbonate can exist in different forms. We can compare the reactions of a lump of calcium carbonate and an equal mass of calcium carbonate powder with equal volumes of dilute hydrochloric acid of the same concentration:

calcium carbonate + hydrochloric acid → calcium chloride + water + carbon dioxide

$$CaCO_3 + 2HCl \rightarrow CaCl_2 + H_2O + CO_2$$

We can measure the volume of gas produced every 30 seconds. The graph in the diagram shows the results of such an experiment.

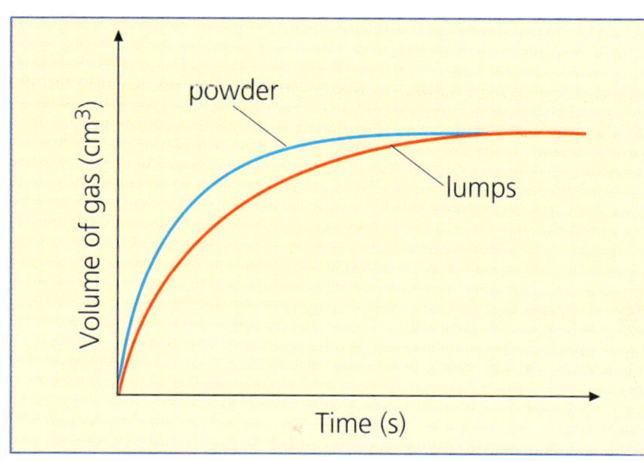

You can see that the same volume of gas is produced in each case because the same quantities of chemicals were used but the time taken is much less with powder – the reaction with the powder is much faster.

Using a catalyst

Some types of filler used to repair damage to car bodies comes in two tubes. When the contents of the two tubes are mixed the filler hardens. One tube contains a **catalyst**.

A catalyst is a substance that changes the rate of a reaction. Usually a catalyst speeds up a chemical reaction but there are some catalysts (called inhibitors) that slow reactions down. Only a small amount of catalyst is usually needed because it is not used up in the reaction.

Hydrogen peroxide is a colourless liquid. It decomposes slowly without a catalyst to form oxygen gas and water. If manganese(IV) oxide is added to hydrogen peroxide the reaction is much faster.

Explaining the rate of a reaction using particles

Substances are made up of **particles**. For a reaction to take place particles have to collide. A reaction gets faster when

- collisions take place more often;
- the colliding particles have more energy, e.g. when they are moving faster.

Increasing concentration

Look at A and B in the diagram on the right. Both boxes contain black and white particles.

Imagine that in both boxes the particles are moving in all directions at the same speed. A reaction takes place whenever the particles collide.

In B the particles are closer together, i.e. the reacting substances are more concentrated. There will be more collisions between black and white in B and therefore a faster reaction.

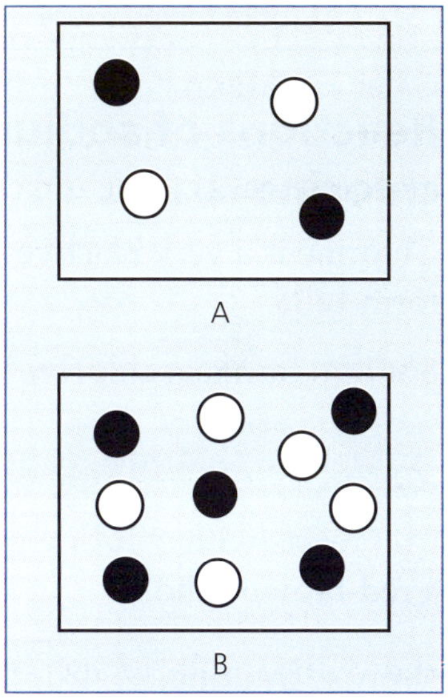

Increasing energy of collisions

Look at A again. When the temperature increases, the black and white particles move faster. The reaction then becomes faster, for two reasons:

- The particles collide more often.
- When the particles collide they have more energy.

Questions

1 What name is given to a substance that speeds up a chemical reaction without being used up?

2 When a reaction is faster, does it take a shorter or longer time?

3 What name is given to a biological catalyst?

4 Why does powdered calcium carbonate react faster with hydrochloric acid than a lump of calcium carbonate?

Properties of the halogens

You need to know

- fluorine, chlorine, bromine and iodine belong to the halogen family;
- patterns in colour, melting points, boiling points and physical states of halogens;
- the reaction of sodium and iron with chlorine;
- the differences in reactivity of the halogens.

As you go down the group from chlorine the halogens become darker in colour. The melting points and boiling points increase down the group. The state changes from gas to solid.

The word halogen means salt producer. The salt sodium chloride is just called salt.

Halogen	Chlorine	Bromine	Iodine
Colour	green	red-brown	grey
Melting point (°C)	−101	−7	114
Boiling point (°C)	−35	58	183
State at room temperature	gas	liquid	solid

Reactions of sodium and iron with chlorine

Chlorine is a very reactive halogen. It reacts with metals to form **salts**.

Sodium burns in **chlorine** to form solid **sodium chloride**:

sodium + chlorine → sodium chloride

Iron reacts with **chlorine** gas to produce **iron(III) chloride**, a red-brown solid.

iron + chlorine → iron(III) chloride

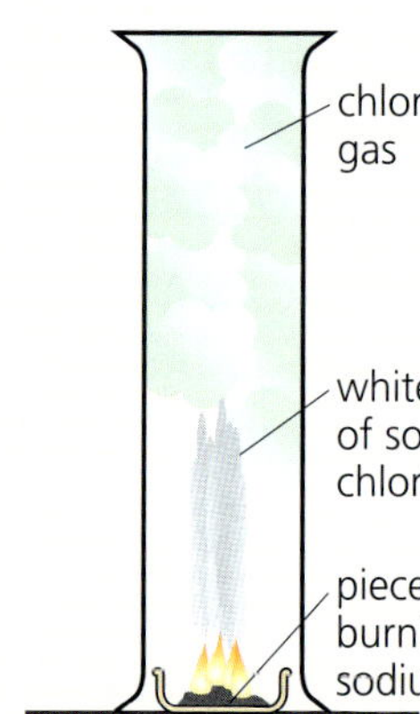

Sodium burning in a gas jar of chlorine

Differences in reactivity of the halogens

The order of reactivity of the three halogens is chlorine (most reactive) > bromine > iodine (least reactive).

Displacement reactions show the differences in reactivity of the halogens.

Potassium and iodine combine in the compound potassium iodide. Chlorine gas added to potassium iodide solution causes a **displacement reaction**.

The reactivity of the halogens decreases down Group 7.

Chlorine, more reactive than iodine, replaces it in the salt **potassium iodide**:

chlorine + potassium iodide → potassium chloride + iodine

Bromine does not react with potassium chloride because bromine is less reactive than chlorine.

A reaction only takes place if the halogen added is more reactive than the halogen already present.

Uses of halogens

The table below summarises the common uses of two halogens – chlorine and iodine.

Halogen	Use	Reason for use
chlorine	purifying water bleaching	kills bacteria that may be harmful household bleach contains chlorine as the active bleaching agent
iodine	as a solution in alcohol to kill bacteria	antiseptic for cuts on the skin

Fluorine is a very reactive gas but fluoride added to water can reduce tooth decay.

Students often think iodine is a liquid because they have seen it in solution.

Questions

1 Which halogen is a liquid at room temperature and atmospheric pressure?
2 Which is the most reactive halogen?
3 What is formed when chlorine is bubbled through potassium bromide solution?
4 What type of reaction is taking place in Question 10?
5 Which halogen is added to water to kill bacteria?

Practice module test

You will have 17 minutes to answer these questions

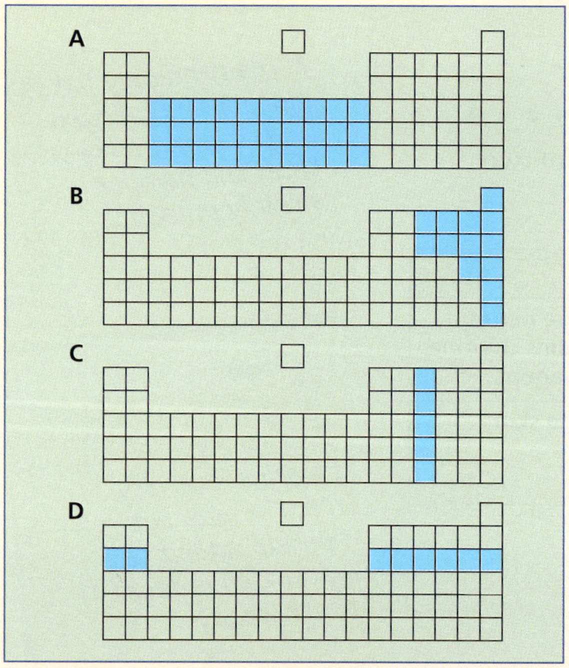

The diagram shows periodic tables with different parts shaded.

1 Which shading shows a period in the periodic table?

2 Which shading shows a group in the periodic table?

3 Which shading shows elements that are gases at room temperature and pressure?

4 Which of the following reactions is the slowest?

- **A** bomb exploding
- **B** candle burning
- **C** gravestone eroding
- **D** tin can rusting

5 In the diagram ● represents

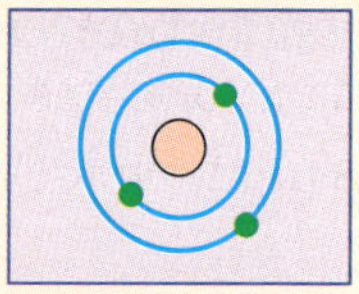

- **A** an electron
- **B** a neutron
- **C** a nucleus
- **D** a proton

6 The elements in the periodic table:

- **A** were discovered by Mendeleev
- **B** are arranged in order of increasing atomic number
- **C** are arranged in order of melting and boiling points
- **D** are arranged in order of decreasing reactivity

7 Sodium reacts with bromine to produce:

- **A** sodium bromide
- **B** sodium bromite
- **C** sodium bromate
- **D** sodium borate

8 Tincture of iodine is a solution of iodine in alcohol. It is used to:

- **A** bleach clothes
- **B** remove stains
- **C** clean cuts and grazes
- **D** unblock sinks and drains

9 In an atom, which particles move around the nucleus?

- **A** protons
- **B** protons and neutrons
- **C** protons and electrons
- **D** electrons

10 A substance that speeds up a chemical reaction without being used up is called a:

- **A** catalyst
- **B** product
- **C** reactant
- **D** solvent

Use the graphs below to answer Questions 11 and 12.

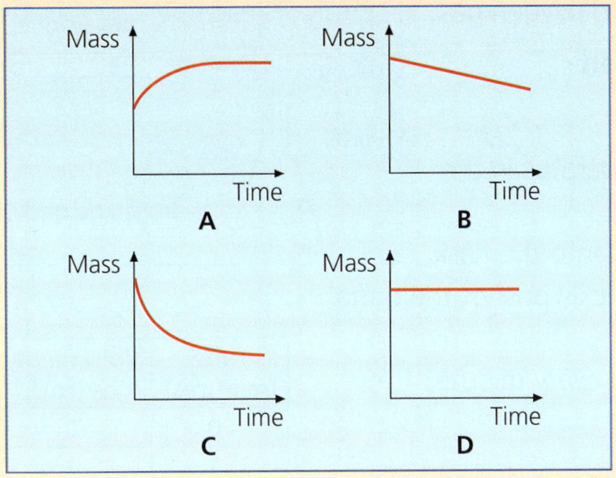

11 Which graph (**A**, **B**, **C** or **D**) shows the mass of calcium carbonate powder with excess dilute hydrochloric acid during the reaction?

12 Manganese(IV) oxide is a catalyst for the decomposition of hydrogen peroxide. Which graph (**A**, **B**, **C** or **D**) shows the mass of manganese(IV) oxide during the reaction?

13 Sodium reacts with chlorine to form sodium chloride. The correct equation for this reaction is:

A $Na + Cl_2 \rightarrow NaCl_2$
B $Na + Cl \rightarrow NaCl$
C $2Na + Cl_2 \rightarrow 2NaCl$
D $2Na + 2Cl \rightarrow (NaCl)_2$

14 Lithium, sodium and potassium are:

A alkali metals
B halogens
C noble gases
D transition metals

15 A reaction between lumps of calcium carbonate can be speeded up by:

A adding water to the hydrochloric acid
B lowering the temperature
C breaking the lumps into smaller pieces
D using half the volume of hydrochloric acid

16 Helium, neon and argon are:

A alkali metals
B halogens
C noble gases
D transition metals

17 Bromine, chlorine and iodine are halogen elements. Which of the following is true?

A they are in Group 1
B they are in Group 2
C they are in Group 7
D they are in Group 8

18 Iron reacts with chlorine to form iron(III) chloride. Which of the following correctly completes the equation: $2Fe + 3Cl_2 \rightarrow$

A $FeCl_3$
B $2FeCl_3$
C Fe_3Cl
D $2Fe_3Cl$

19 Lithium and sodium are elements in the same group of the periodic table. They must:

A have the same number of electrons in the outer shell
B be found in the same ore
C have the same reaction with cold water
D form coloured compounds

20 Which of the following pairs of substances will react?

A potassium chloride and bromine
B potassium chloride and iodine
C potassium bromide and iodine
D potassium bromide and chlorine

Answers to these questions can be found on pages 140–144

Getting it right

1 Hydrogen peroxide decomposes into water and oxygen gas.

hydrogen peroxide → water + oxygen

$2H_2O_2(aq) \rightarrow 2H_2O(l) + O_2(g)$

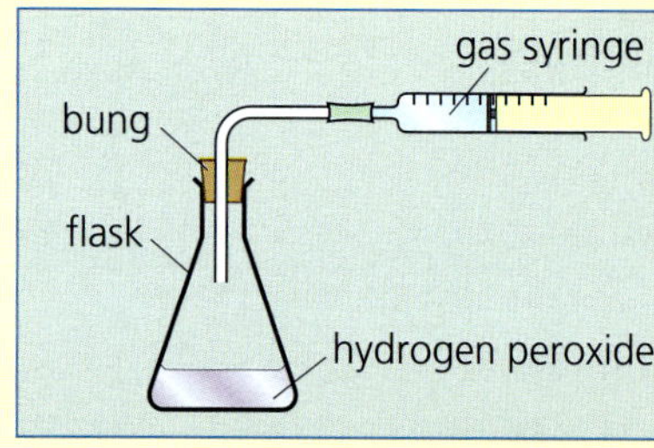

Bobby carries out an experiment using the apparatus in the diagram.

He puts 50 cm^3 of hydrogen peroxide solution into the flask.

He adds 0.5 g of manganese(IV) oxide and quickly pushes the bung into the flask.

He measures the total volume of gas collected every minute.

His results are shown in the table.

Time (minutes)	Volume of gas (cm^3)
0	0
1	1
2	20
3	33
4	45
5	53
6	59
7	60
8	60
9	60
10	60

(a) Draw a graph of Bobby's results on the grid provided.

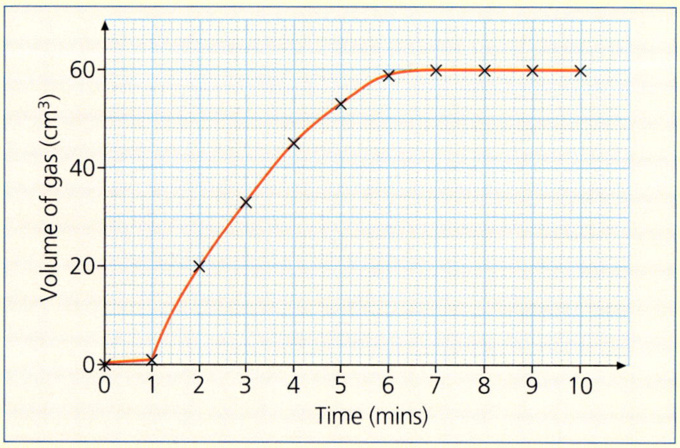

[3]

There are two marks for correct plotting and one for drawing the best line.

(b) After how many minutes is the reaction finished?

7 minutes **[1]**

(c) Bobby repeats the experiment but puts 50 cm^3 of water into the flask before adding the manganese(IV) oxide. On the same grid sketch the graph he would get this time. **[2]**

(d) Bobby wants to investigate whether the quantity of manganese(IV) oxide used affects the rate of reaction. Explain how he should do this. **[5]**

Repeat using 5 different masses of manganesel (V) oxide. Same volume of hydrogen peroxide each time. Same concentration of hydrogen peroxide. Same temperature. Measure the volume of gas collected at intervals each time. Plot graphs – the steeper the graph the faster the reaction.

There are six marking points given. Four marks are awarded for any four of these. An additional QWC mark is available if you ensure that spelling, punctuation and grammar are accurate so that the meaning is clear. Candidates often do not give enough detail in their answers.

Chemistry in action

This module is about crude oil and the materials made from it.

Crude oil has formed in the Earth over millions of years.
After extraction, crude oil has to be refined by fractional distillation to make it into different fractions, with different boiling point ranges and different uses. Hydrocarbons produced from crude oil are commonly used as fuels.

Plastics or polymers are made from crude oil and have a wide range of uses. They are made by the polymerisation of alkenes, a type of hydrocarbon. Alkenes are produced by cracking long chain alkanes

Crude oil

You need to know

- how crude oil was formed in the Earth;
- that crude oil is a mixture of hydrocarbons;
- that hydrocarbons are compounds of hydrogen and carbon only;
- that crude oil can be separated into fractions by fractional distillation and that each fraction has a different use;
- that the properties of a fraction are related to the size of its molecules.

How was crude oil formed?

Over millions of years, small animal organisms have died and decayed inside the Earth, forming a black sticky liquid that we call **crude oil**. This process required **high temperatures** (between 90 and 120°C), **high pressure** and the **absence of oxygen**.

The crude oil is trapped in porous rocks between layers of impervious rock that prevent the oil from escaping.

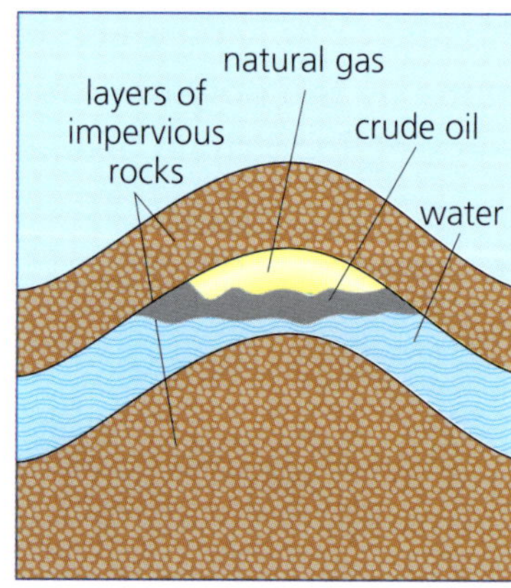

Crude oil trapped in rock layers in the Earth

Crude oil is a mixture of hydrocarbons

Crude oil is a complex mixture made up of different **compounds**. Most of these compounds are **hydrocarbons**. A hydrocarbon is a compound of carbon and hydrogen **only**. This mixture of hydrocarbons is of little use until the crude oil is refined.

A compound is formed when atoms of different elements combine in fixed numbers, e.g. water (H_2O) is a compound of hydrogen and oxygen – two atoms of hydrogen and one of oxygen.

Crude oil can be separated by fractional distillation

We use oil refineries to produce useful materials from crude oil by a process called **fractional distillation**.

Fractional distillation of crude oil involves separating the oil into different fractions, each having a different boiling point range.

The crude oil is boiled and the **vapour** formed enters a tall column. As the vapour passes up the tower, different compounds condense at different levels, depending upon their boiling point.

Compounds with high boiling points condense quickly, low down in the column. Compounds with low boiling points condense much further up the column where the temperature is lower.

The diagram shows the fractional distillation of crude oil and some of the different fractions produced.

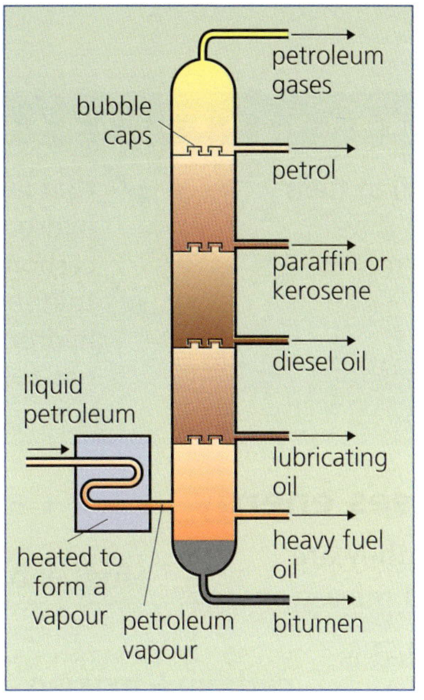

Fractional distillation column

Try to draw a fractionating column without looking at the book.

Try to write down a list of five fractions obtained from crude oil, giving a use for each.

Fraction	Boiling point range (°C)	Number of carbon atoms	Uses
refinery gases	up to 40	1–4	fuel
petrol (gasoline)	40–140	5–10	fuel for cars
kerosene (paraffin)	140–180	8–12	fuel for aeroplanes
diesel oil	180–250	10–20	fuel for lorries and buses
fuel oil	250–340	20–40	fuel for central heating, ships
bitumen	over 340		tar for surfacing roads

The properties of each fraction depend upon the size of its molecules. The table shows that the boiling point increases as the molecules become larger (i.e. have more carbon atoms). Other properties of the various fractions also depend on the size of their molecules – for example, how easily they catch alight or how easily they pour.

Questions

1. Which two elements are combined in a hydrocarbon?
2. What process is used in an oil refinery to make crude oil into useful products?
3. What three conditions were needed to turn small living organisms into crude oil?
4. Are compounds with low boiling point run off near the top or near the bottom of the tower in an oil refinery?

Burning fuels

You need to know

- that burning (or combustion) of fuels releases energy;
- that the addition of oxygen makes this an **oxidation** reaction;
- that complete combustion of hydrocarbons produces carbon dioxide and water;
- that incomplete combustion of hydrocarbons produces carbon and carbon monoxide (a toxic gas);
- that incomplete combustion of hydrocarbons can happen in faulty gas appliances.

Burning of fuels releases energy

Hydrocarbons are **fuels**. When they are burned they use up oxygen and release energy:

fuel + oxygen → products + energy

A reaction where oxygen is added is an oxidation reaction, for example

carbon + oxygen → carbon dioxide

It is called oxidation because oxygen is added.

The products of combustion

The products of combustion (burning) depend upon the amount of air or oxygen present.

Complete combustion takes place when the fuel burns in a plentiful supply of air, i.e. there is an excess. It releases the maximum amount of energy. The products are **carbon dioxide** and **water**:

Excess means that there is more than enough oxygen for the reaction to take place.

fuel + excess oxygen → carbon dioxide + water + energy

When there is a limited amount of air or oxygen, we get **incomplete combustion**. Products include **carbon** (usually as soot) and **carbon monoxide**.

Carbon monoxide is a **toxic** gas. It is also colourless and odourless.

Incomplete combustion can be dangerous

Burning a hydrocarbon can produce poisonous carbon monoxide. This happens if the combustion is incomplete because not enough air reaches the burner. Every year about 50 people die of carbon monoxide poisoning in the UK.

Questions

1 The simplest hydrocarbon contains one carbon and four hydrogen atoms in each molecule. What is the name of this hydrocarbon?

2 What two substances are produced when natural gas burns in a plentiful supply of air?

3 What is the name of the poisonous gas produced when natural gas burns in a limited supply of air?

Plastics

You need to know

- that methane, ethane, propane and butane are the first four members of a family of hydrocarbons;
- polymers are long chain molecules made up of large numbers of smaller molecules called monomers joined together – monomer molecules are unsaturated;
- polymers (the chemical name for plastics) have many uses;
- polymers do not easily rot away and so there are problems with their disposal.

Families of hydrocarbons

Hydrocarbons exist in different families. One family is called **alkanes**. The simplest hydrocarbon in this family is **methane**. This has molecules with one carbon atom attached to four hydrogen atoms.

The next three members of the alkane family are:

C_2H_6 ethane; C_3H_8 propane, C_4H_{10} butane

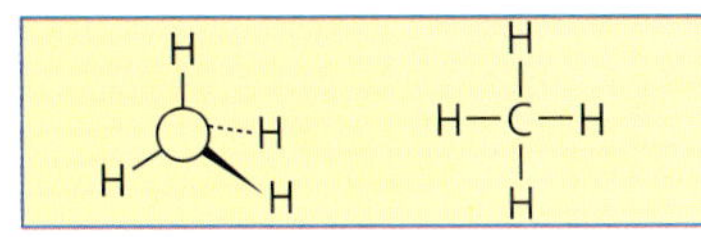

Structure of methane

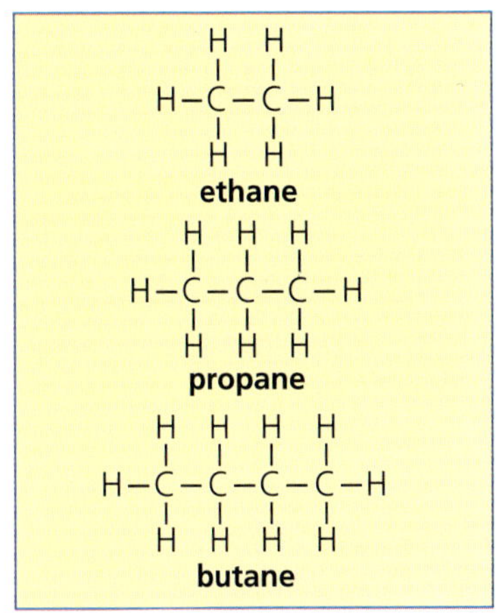

Structure of ethane, propane and butane

Polymers and their applications

Fractions from crude oil are the starting materials for making polymers.

Polymers are long chain molecules, formed when thousands of small units called **monomers** join together. Polymers have replaced materials such as metals and wood in many applications.

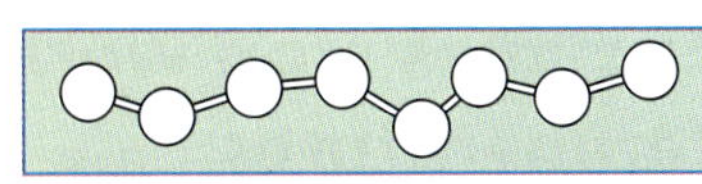

A polymer chain

Problems disposing of polymers

Polymers can cause litter problems because, unlike paper and cardboard, they do not rot away. They can be **recycled**, but this is often not economic.

When they are burned, polymers can form poisonous products such as carbon monoxide and hydrogen chloride (from PVC).

Polymer	Elements present	Uses
poly(ethene)	carbon and hydrogen	milk crates, cling film, dustbin bags, food storage boxes
poly(propene)	carbon and hydrogen	washing up bowls
poly(styrene)	carbon and hydrogen	flowerpots, ceiling tiles, plastic model kits
poly(chloroethene) or PVC	carbon, hydrogen and chlorine	insulation for electricity cables, guttering

Questions

1 Which family of hydrocarbons includes methane, ethane and propane?

2 Butane contains four carbon atoms. How many hydrogen atoms does it contain?

Enzymes

You need to know

- that enzymes are biological catalysts;
- about the uses of enzymes at home and in industry;
- that enzymes stop working at high temperatures.

Uses of enzymes at home and in industry

Enzymes in yeast ferment sugars to produce beer and wine. The enzymes act on sugar and turn it into ethanol and carbon dioxide:

A catalyst is a substance that speeds up the rate of a chemical reaction.

sugar + water → ethanol + carbon dioxide

A loaf of bread left to stand before baking will rise. The loaf rises as the above reaction produces bubbles of carbon dioxide, making the dough expand.

Biological washing powders are washing powders that contain enzymes. They are good at removing stains in cool water. The enzymes act on the stains and break them down.

Enzymes acting on milk produce cheese and yoghurt. Injecting hard centred chocolates with the enzyme invertase makes soft centred chocolates.

Enzymes stop working at high temperatures

Enzyme reactions such as these work best at temperatures around 35°C. At higher temperatures the enzymes are broken down or **denatured**.

Students often write that enzymes are killed at high temperatures – this is incorrect.

Questions

1 Write down the name of the gas formed when enzymes act on sugar solution.

2 Which of the following are produced using enzymes?

cheese coffee soap yoghurt

Types of chemical reactions

You need to know

- ✔ that reactions of acids with bases or alkalis to produce **salts** are called **neutralisation** reactions.
- ✔ that a **thermal decomposition** reaction is where heating splits up a substance;
- ✔ that limewater is produced by reacting calcium oxide with water;
- ✔ that calcium carbonate is used to produce glass, cement and iron.

Combustion (or burning), **oxidation** (where oxygen is added) and **reduction** (where oxidation is removed) are types of reaction.

Neutralisation reactions

acid + base (or alkali) → salt + water

Salt and water are produced in a neutralisation reaction.

For example:

sulphuric acid + sodium hydroxide → sodium sulphate + water

Sometimes the salt produced can be added to soil as a **fertiliser**.

Calcium oxide and calcium hydroxide are both alkaline and can be added to soil to neutralise the acidity.

Plants need large quantities of the elements nitrogen, potassium and phosphorus to be healthy.

Thermal decomposition

The splitting up of a substance into simpler products by heating is called **thermal decomposition.**

calcium carbonate → calcium oxide + carbon dioxide

copper carbonate → copper oxide + carbon dioxide
green powder black powder

Uses of calcium carbonate

Product	Other materials needed	Summary of process
glass	sodium carbonate and sand	melting the mixture together
cement	clay	heating limestone powder and clay and grinding the mixture to a powder
iron	iron ore and coke	heated in a furnace with blasts of hot air

Questions

Ammonium sulphate is a salt produced from ammonia.

1 Write down the name of the acid used to make ammonium sulphate.

2 Suggest one use of ammonium sulphate.

Practice module test

You will have 17 minutes to answer these questions

1 Poly(ethene) is a polymer. Which of the following could it be used to make?

- **A** a carrier bag
- **B** a saucepan
- **C** an electricity cable
- **D** a crane

2 Ammonium sulphate, ammonium nitrate and potassium nitrate are all salts that can be used as:

- **A** acids
- **B** alkalis
- **C** fertilisers
- **D** plastics

3 The chemical formula for calcium carbonate is:

- **A** $CaCO$
- **B** $CaCO_3$
- **C** CaC_2
- **D** CaC_3O

4 Limestone is used to make:

- **A** glass
- **B** plastic
- **C** bread
- **D** cheese

5 A gas fire needs to be checked regularly to see if:

- **A** there is enough air to burn the gas
- **B** the temperature of the flame is correct
- **C** it is burning enough gas
- **D** it is burning quietly

6 Beer, yoghurt and cheese are all made using:

- **A** acids
- **B** alkalis
- **C** enzymes
- **D** salt

7 Crude oil is a source of:

- **A** acids
- **B** alkalis
- **C** fuels
- **D** salts

8 Complete combustion takes place when:

- **A** no air is present
- **B** a limited amount of air is produced
- **C** there is no ventilation
- **D** a plentiful supply of air is present

9 Which fraction is suitable for jet engine fuel?

- **A** bitumen
- **B** crude oil
- **C** fuel oil
- **D** kerosene

10 Fertilisers are produced by:

- **A** cracking
- **B** decomposition
- **C** fractional distillation
- **D** neutralisation

11 Crude oil was formed from small animals that lived in the sea. When they died their bodies were covered with layers of rock, which kept out air. What other conditions were needed to turn these into crude oil?

- **A** high pressures and low temperatures
- **B** low pressures and low temperatures
- **C** high pressures and high temperatures
- **D** low pressures and high temperatures

12 Which of the following word equations represents neutralisation?

- **A** lead carbonate → lead oxide + carbon dioxide
- **B** lead oxide + nitric acid → lead nitrate + water
- **C** lead nitrate → lead oxide + nitrogen dioxide + oxygen
- **D** lead oxide + carbon → lead + carbon monoxide

13 Which one of the following is a hydrocarbon?

- **A** C_6H_6
- **B** CO
- **C** C_2H_3Cl
- **D** $C_6H_{12}O_6$

14 Four fractions obtained from crude oil are bitumen, diesel, kerosene and petrol. In which list are the four fractions in order of increasing boiling point?

- **A** bitumen, diesel, petrol, kerosene
- **B** petrol, diesel, kerosene, bitumen
- **C** diesel, kerosene, petrol, bitumen
- **D** petrol, kerosene, diesel, bitumen

15 Which gas could be produced when poly(vinylchloride) or PVC is burned but not when poly(ethene) is burnt?

- **A** carbon dioxide
- **B** carbon monoxide
- **C** hydrogen chloride
- **D** water

16 An alkene contains:

- **A** only single bonds
- **B** a double bond and single bonds
- **C** only double bonds
- **D** a single bond and double bonds

17 Which word equation represents fermentation?

- **A** sugar + oxygen → carbon dioxide + water
- **B** water + carbon dioxide → sugar + oxygen
- **C** sugar + water → ethanol + carbon dioxide
- **D** ethanol + oxygen → carbon dioxide + water

18 Crude oil was made from small marine organisms under the effect of:

- **A** high temperature, high pressure and lack of oxygen
- **B** low temperature, high pressure and lack of oxygen
- **C** high temperature, low pressure and presence of oxygen
- **D** low temperature, low pressure and presence of oxygen

19 Which gas is produced when a hydrocarbon burns in a limited supply of air but not in a plentiful supply of air?

- **A** carbon dioxide
- **B** carbon monoxide
- **C** oxygen
- **D** steam

20 Methane is a:

- **A** compound of carbon, hydrogen and oxygen
- **B** compound of carbon and hydrogen
- **C** mixture of carbon and hydrogen
- **D** mixture of carbon and water

Answers to these questions can be found on pages 140–144

Getting it right

1 A plastic called PVC is now used to make plastic guttering and drainpipes for houses.

(a) Choose one material from the list that was commonly used for this purpose before PVC was discovered.

cardboard   cast iron   lead   wood

cast iron **[1]**

(b) Suggest two advantages of PVC for this purpose.

PVC has a lower density so needs less support.
PVC does not rot away.

[2]

Do not write that PVC is cheaper. You have no idea of costs. Cost is not usually an accepted answer. Other answers could include that PVC is easily moulded or can be produced in different colours.

2 The rubbish collected in Anytown is burned in a large incinerator. The energy released in this process is used to provide hot water for neighbouring houses. Some of the rubbish consists of hydrocarbons.

(a) Write down the names of the two elements combined in all hydrocarbons.

carbon and hydrogen **[1]**

(b) Suggest one reason why rubbish should be burned in a plentiful supply of air in the incinerator.

To avoid carbon monoxide being formed, which is poisonous.

[2]

In Brentown, the rubbish is buried underground in a landfill site. Over a number of years the rubbish breaks down and methane gas is produced. This gas is collected and burned on the site.

(c) Write a balanced equation for the burning of methane is excess air.

$CH_4 + 2O_2 \rightarrow CO_2 + 2H_2O$ **[3]**

The three marks here are for the correct formulae on the left-hand side, correct formulae on the right-hand side and for balancing the equation.

(d) Why is this gas collected and burned?

Mixtures of methane and air can explode.
Collecting and burning it prevents this.

[2]

Apart from the risk of explosion, methane is a major greenhouse gas and it would further global warming.

(e) Suggest one reason why the disposal of rubbish in Anytown is better than in Brentown.

Energy released is used rather than wasted.

[1]

Energy and electricity

This module is about electricity and energy resources. The first topic in the module covers circuits and how the current in a circuit is affected by the voltage and different circuit components.

Using electricity from the mains safely is the subject of the second topic in the module. The final topic is concerned with generating electricity from different resources and how to insulate buildings to conserve energy resources.

Circuits

You need to know

- about resistance and how it affects the current in a circuit;
- how the voltage across a component depends on its resistance and the current passing in it;
- how the current in a fixed resistor, a filament lamp and a diode depends on the voltage;
- how the resistance of a light-dependent resistor and a thermistor depend on the light intensity and temperature.

Direct and alternating currents

Electric **current** is a flow of charged particles. Cells and batteries cause a **direct current**, one that passes in the same direction all the time. The current from the mains supply is **alternating current** – it changes direction .

Any electric current that changes direction is an alternating current.

Units are important

The size of the current (measured in amps, A) in a circuit depends on the **resistance** (measured in ohms, Ω) and the **voltage** (measured in volts, V). Resistance is a measure of the opposition to current passing in a circuit. The greater the resistance, the smaller the current:

- Increasing the resistance in a circuit decreases the current.
- Increasing the voltage causes the current to increase.

The voltage and the amount of resistance in a circuit determine the size of the current that passes.

The relationship between voltage, current and resistance is:

voltage = current × resistance or $V = I \times R$

You need to know how the current in three common circuit components changes when the applied voltage is changed:

- The current in a **fixed resistor** is proportional to the voltage. The resistance has a constant value.
- The current in a **filament lamp** increases when the voltage is increased, but not in proportion – the resistance of the filament increases as it gets hotter.
- The current in a **diode** can only pass in one direction (shown by the direction of the arrow on the circuit symbol); the diode only conducts when a minimum voltage (about 0.6 V) is reached – after this its resistance decreases as the voltage is increased.

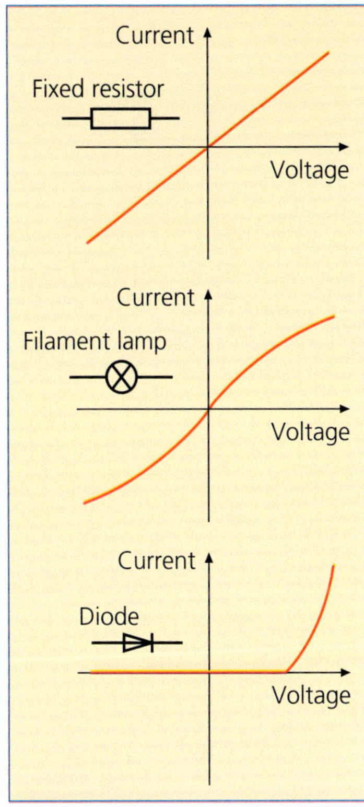

Light-dependent resistors (LDRs) are used in circuits that switch lights on automatically after dusk. **Thermistors** (temperature-dependent resistors) are used to switch the heaters in incubators on and off to maintain a constant temperature. The resistance of these components depends on the environmental conditions:

- the resistance of an LDR decreases when the light becomes brighter;
- the resistance of a thermistor decreases when its temperature increases.

The more energy being supplied from the environment to the component, the greater the current that passes.

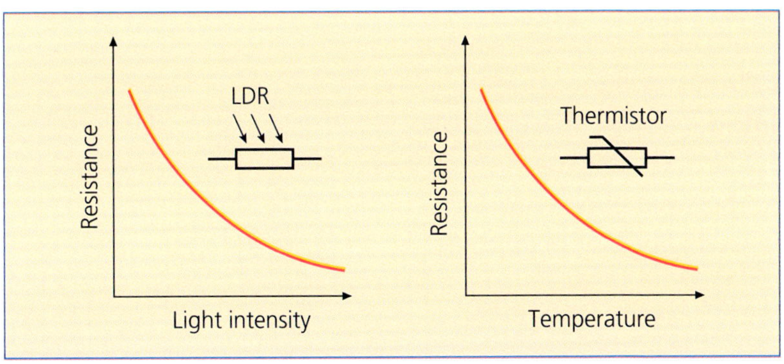

Questions

1. What is the difference between alternating and direct current?
2. Should a voltmeter be connected in series or in parallel with a component?
3. The current in a 4.0 Ω resistor is 2.5 A. Calculate the voltage across the resistor.
4. Which component has a resistance that goes down when the light gets brighter?

Mains electricity

You need to know

- ✔ how appliances are connected safely to the mains supply;
- ✔ the job of each conductor in a mains lead;
- ✔ that electric current causes heating and how this is used in domestic appliances;
- ✔ how to calculate the cost of energy from the mains supply.

The mains supply to a house and to a domestic appliance uses three conductors:

- The live wire is the high-voltage conductor. It carries the energy to the house or appliance.
- The neutral wire is there to complete the circuit.
- The earth wire is for safety. It prevents the casing of the appliance from becoming live.

The diagram shows the colours of the insulation used on the wires in a flexible cable connected to a plug.

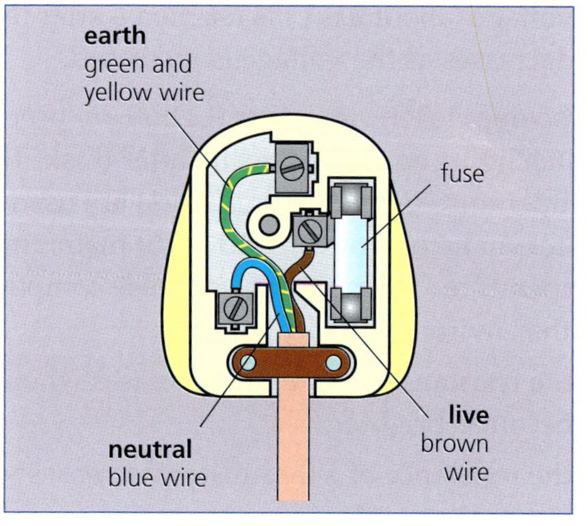

Appliances that have a plastic casing and no metal exposed parts do not need an earth wire. These appliances are described as being **double insulated**, because there are two layers of insulation between the user and the live conductor. The plastic case cannot become live because it is not a conductor, so it provides an extra layer of insulation.

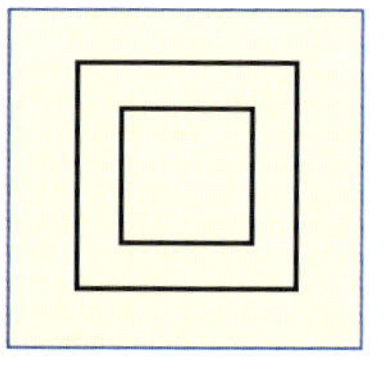

This symbol shows that an appliance is double insulated

The electricity supply entering a house passes through a consumer unit. In a house, each circuit is protected by a fuse or circuit breaker.

A fuse:

- consists of a thin wire that is heated by the current passing in it;
- melts and breaks the circuit when an excessive current passes;
- needs to be replaced by a new piece of wire of the correct rating when a fault has occurred and been repaired;
- is always fitted to the live conductor.

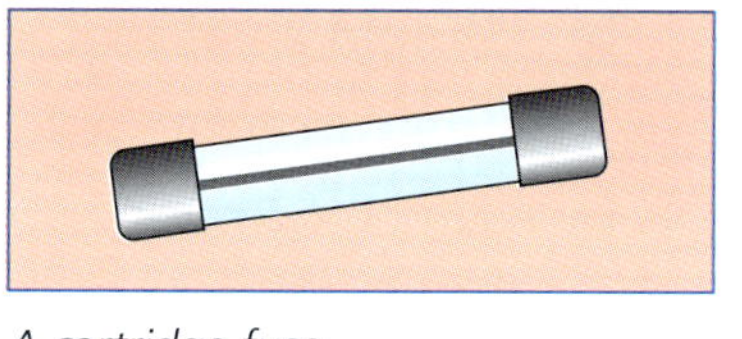

A cartridge fuse

Domestic appliances transfer energy from electricity into **heat**, **light** and **movement** (including sound).

Remember that sound is carried by the movement of particles.

Whenever a current passes in a resistor, heat is produced. When an electric current passes in an appliance, there is always some heating because of the resistance of the wires.

Some appliances are designed to transfer energy from the electricity supply to heat. These include:

- Electric bar heaters: the elements become hot and transfer energy by **electromagnetic radiation** to the surroundings.
- Immersion heaters: these heat the water in the hot water tank. The hot water moves around the tank by **convection currents**.
- Kettles, cookers and irons: these devices all use the heating effect of a current to raise the temperature of a heating element; in turn this heats the surroundings by transferring energy by convection currents and conduction. For example, an iron heats your clothes by transferring energy by conduction through the metal plate.

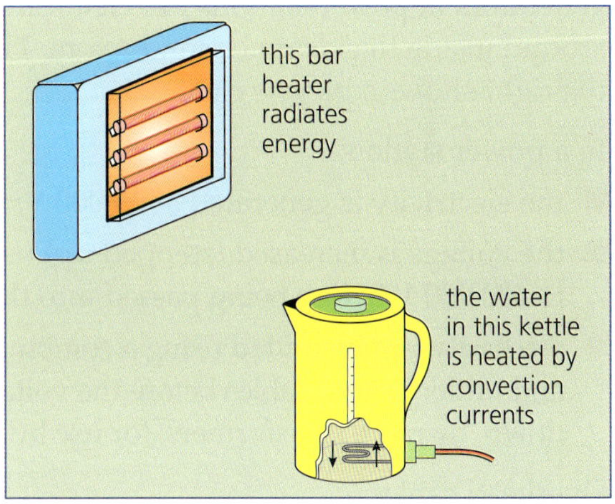

Electricity supply companies charge for the energy transferred from the mains supply to a home or workplace.

The energy is measured in **kilowatt-hours** (kW h), the amount of energy transferred by a 1 kW appliance in 1 hour.

The cost of this energy transfer can be calculated using the relationship:

cost = power in kW × time in h × cost of 1 kWh

This relationship will always be given if required in module tests or exam.

Questions

1 In which conductor in a mains connecting lead is the fuse placed?

2 Which of the conductors in a mains connecting lead normally carries no current?

3 What happens to the fuse wire when a fuse 'blows'?

Energy resources and transfer

You need to know

- ✔ how electricity is generated;
- ✔ about the use of transformers in distributing electricity;
- ✔ the environmental implications of generating electricity using renewable and non-renewable resources;
- ✔ how insulation uses trapped air to reduce the energy transfer between objects at different temperatures.

Electricity is generated by the rotation of a magnet within, or next to, a coil of wire. A small generator such as a bicycle dynamo uses a permanent magnet, but the generators in power stations use electromagnets that spin around inside thick copper conductors. The diagram on the right shows a bicycle dynamo.

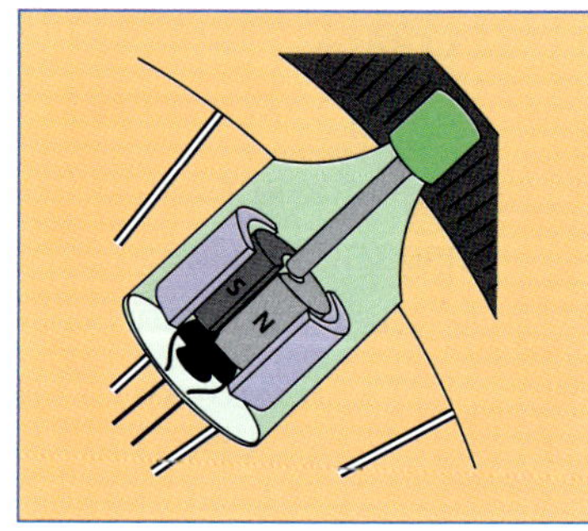

A bicycle dynamo

In a power station:

- the electricity is generated at 25 000 V;
- the voltage is increased (stepped up) using transformers to 400 000 V before being passed into the grid network;
- electricity is transmitted using a combination of overhead and underground cables before the voltage is stepped down, by more transformers, for use by consumers.

Overhead cables:

- are cheap to install and to operate because they are cooled by convection currents in the surrounding air;
- are damaged easily in storms and windy weather;
- can be repaired quickly because the damage can be seen easily;
- are ugly and can spoil areas of natural beauty.

Underground cables:

- are more expensive to install than overhead cables;
- need a flow of coolant to remove excess heat;
- are more costly to repair than overhead cables because damage cannot be detected easily.

The air acts as a coolant and provides good electrical insulation between overhead cables and the ground

Currently, the burning of fossil fuels such as coal and gas generates most of the UK's electricity supply. Fossil fuels are being used up rapidly and when they are burned they produce carbon dioxide (a greenhouse gas) and sulphur dioxide (which produces acid rain).

In the future we will need to use renewable sources of energy to generate electricity. These include:

- Wind – large wind farms could be built offshore where the wind is reliable, there is plenty of room and the noise does not cause a nuisance.
- Tides – a reliable, cost-effective generator of electricity from tidal flow has yet to be developed.
- Solar panels – these can be used to heat domestic water and to generate electricity directly.

Each wind turbine can generate 400 kW of electricity – enough for the needs of a small village of a few hundred people

There are plans to build large offshore wind farms off the east coast of England. These would be out of sight and hearing.

The amount of polluting gases emitted from power stations can be reduced if there is less demand for electricity. This can be achieved by:

- using low-power appliances such as fluorescent lamps in place of filament lamps.
- improving the insulation of homes and workplaces.

Keeping the heat in

For most of the year, the temperature inside your house is kept at a higher level than the temperature outside, possibly by central heating. This results in a flow of heat from the inside of your house to the outside because of the difference in temperature (as shown in the diagram). The amount of energy flow can be reduced in several ways:

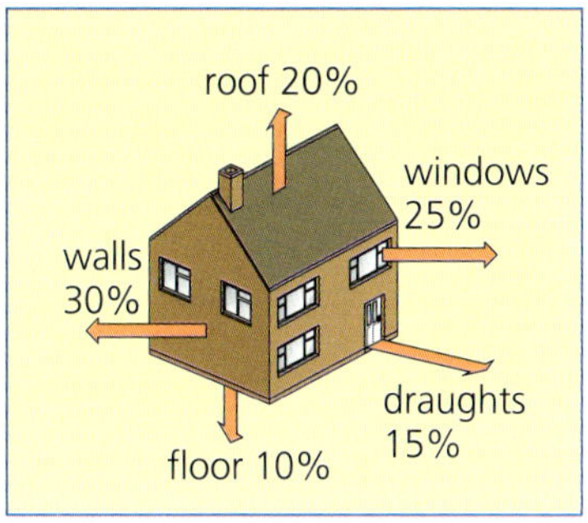

- **loft insulation** reduces the energy conducted through bedroom ceilings and convected through the air space in a loft.
- **double glazing** reduces the energy conducted through windows.
- **cavity wall insulation** stops energy transfer by convection currents between the inner and outer walls of a house.

Energy can still flow through an insulated cavity wall by conduction

Questions

1. How are electromagnets used to generate electricity in a power station?
2. What devices are used to change the voltage of mains electricity?
3. What type of fuel are coal, oil and gas?
4. What is used to reduce the energy loss through the walls of a house?

Practice module test

You will have 17 minutes to answer these questions

1 In the circuit below, component V is a

- **A** lamp
- **B** diode
- **C** thermistor
- **D** variable resistor

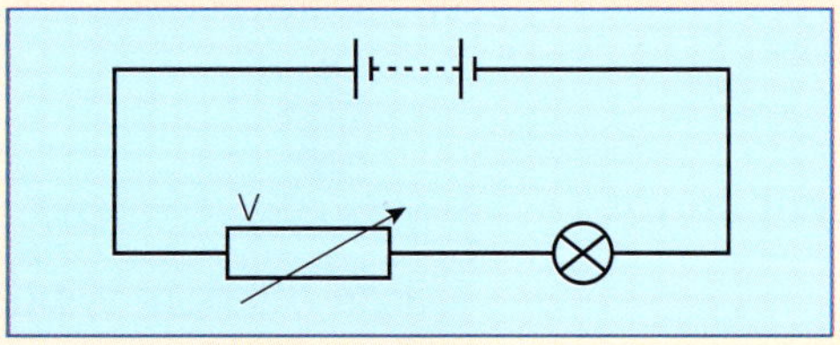

2 In the circuit below, which voltmeter (**A**, **B**, **C** or **D**) is in the correct position to measure the voltage across the battery?

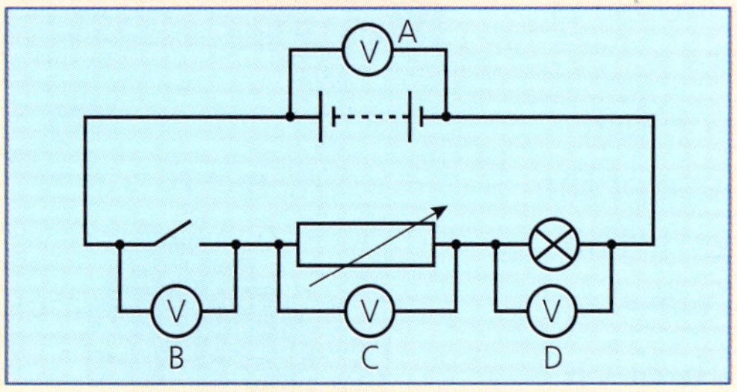

3 When the resistance of a circuit is increased, the current:

- **A** decreases
- **B** increases
- **C** stays the same
- **D** stops

4 The resistance of a light-dependent resistor (LDR) increases when:

- **A** the temperature increases
- **B** the temperature decreases
- **C** the light intensity increases
- **D** the light intensity decreases

5 The current from a battery is:

- **A** alternating current
- **B** direct current
- **C** longitudinal current
- **D** transverse current

6 In a correctly wired plug, the colour of the insulation on the live wire is:

- **A** blue
- **B** brown
- **C** green
- **D** yellow

7 Bar heaters, immersion heaters and kettles all rely on the fact that an electric current causes:

- **A** cooling
- **B** heating
- **C** magnetism
- **D** movement

8 The symbol below means that an appliance:

- **A** must have an earth wire
- **B** is single insulated
- **C** is double insulated
- **D** is triple insulated

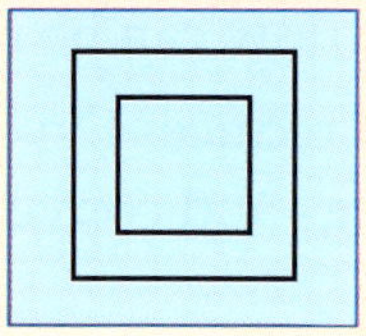

9 The energy transferred from the mains electricity supply is measured in:

- **A** joules
- **B** watts
- **C** kilowatts
- **D** kilowatt-hours

10 One advantage of using underground rather than overhead cables to distribute electricity is that:

- **A** they are cheap to install
- **B** running costs are low
- **C** overhead cables are unsightly
- **D** they cannot interfere with buildings

11 Which part of a cycle dynamo rotates when it generates electricity?

- **A** the electromagnet
- **B** the permanent magnet
- **C** the temporary magnet
- **D** the coil of wire

12 Which line on the graph (**A**, **B**, **C** or **D**) shows a direct current?

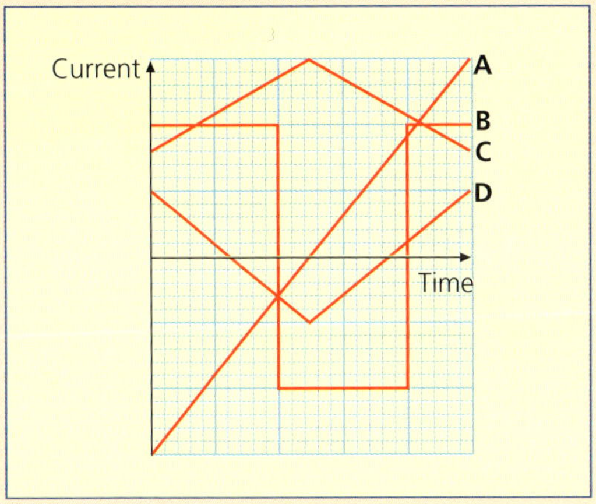

13 A diode:

- **A** allows current to pass in both directions at once
- **B** allows current to pass in one direction only
- **C** only allows alternating current to pass
- **D** does not allow direct current to pass

14 The colour of the insulation on the earth wire in a correctly wired plug is:

- **A** brown
- **B** brown and yellow
- **C** green
- **D** green and yellow

15 An appliance that is double insulated:

- **A** does not need a live wire
- **B** does not need a neutral wire
- **C** does not need an earth wire
- **D** does not need a fuse

16 A transformer can be used to:

- **A** generate a direct voltage
- **B** generate an alternating voltage
- **C** change the size of a direct voltage
- **D** change the size of an alternating voltage

Questions 17 to 19

Here are some methods used to insulate a home:

- **A** cavity wall insulation
- **B** double glazing
- **C** draught-proofing
- **D** loft insulation

17 Which of these methods reduces the energy lost through a bedroom ceiling?

18 Which of these reduces the energy lost through the walls?

19 Which of these reduces the energy lost through the windows?

20 The energy input to a wind generator is:

- **A** gravitational energy
- **B** kinetic energy
- **C** potential energy
- **D** pressure energy

Answers to these questions can be found on pages 140–144

Getting it right

1 (a) The lead connecting a metal-cased kettle to the mains supply contains three conductors. The colours of the insulation on these conductors are brown, blue and green/yellow.

(i) What colour is the insulation on the conductor that carries energy into the house?

Brown **[1]**

(ii) What colour is the insulation on the conductor that should be connected to the metal casing of the kettle?

Green/yellow **[1]**

(iii) What colour is the insulation on the live wire?

Brown **[1]**

(iv) Which colour conductor, together with the fuse, protects the user from electrocution?

Green/yellow **[1]**

> The question asks for the colour of the conductor so the answer 'live', although true, would not be acceptable.

(b) (i) In normal use, the current in a kettle element is 10 A. Which of the following fuses should be fitted to the plug?

1 A 3 A 5 A 13 A

Explain why the others are not suitable.

13A, as the others would "blow" with a current of 10A

[2]

> Usually an appliance should be fitted with a fuse that has a slightly higher rating than the current that passes when it operates normally.

(ii) What happens to a fuse when too great a current passes in it?

The wire melts and breaks the circuit.

[2]

(c) A kettle has a power of 2.4 kW. The cost of energy from electricity is 7p/kW h. Use the relationship:

cost = power × time × cost in kW h

to calculate the cost of using the kettle for a total of 2 hours each day for a week.

cost = 2.4 x 14 x 7p = 235.2p **[2]**

> When answering questions of this type, you do not have to change the final answer into pounds, but if you do, then make sure you do it correctly.

Waves, space and atoms

The title of this module describes the three topics in it. The waves section concentrates on the use of the waves making up the electromagnetic spectrum. Electromagnetic waves are used to gather evidence and information about space, the subject of the second topic. The final topic is about radioactivity – its existence, benefits and dangers.

Waves

You need to know

- ✔ what the difference is between a longitudinal and a transverse wave, and how to describe both of them;
- ✔ the meaning of the terms **frequency**, **wavelength** and **amplitude**;
- ✔ the order of the electromagnetic spectrum and how to describe the uses and hazards of each group of waves;
- ✔ about the cause and effects of refraction;
- ✔ about **ultrasound** and its uses.

There are two types of waves:

- In a **longitudinal wave** the vibrations are parallel to the direction of wave travel.
- In a **transverse wave** the vibrations are at right angles to the direction of wave travel.

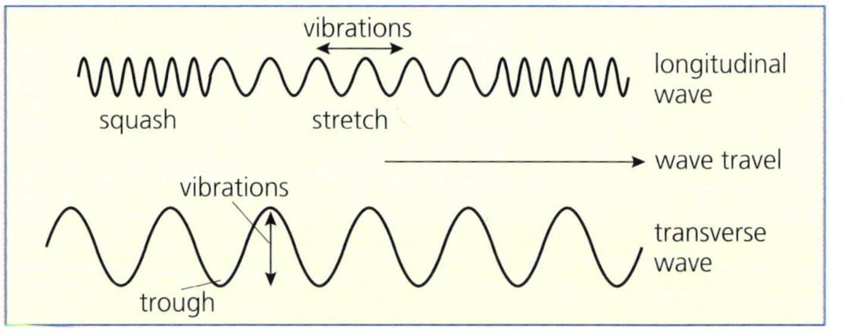

Vibrations in longitudinal and transverse waves

Wave measurements that are common to both types of wave are:

- Frequency (symbol f) – the number of waves occurring each second. Frequency is measured in Hertz (Hz).
- Wavelength (symbol λ) – the length of one cycle of a wave. Wavelength is measured in metres (m).
- Amplitude (symbol a) – the greatest displacement from the normal position. Amplitude is also measured in metres (m).

One cycle of a longitudinal wave is made up of a squash and a stretch. For a transverse wave the cycle is made up of a trough and a crest.

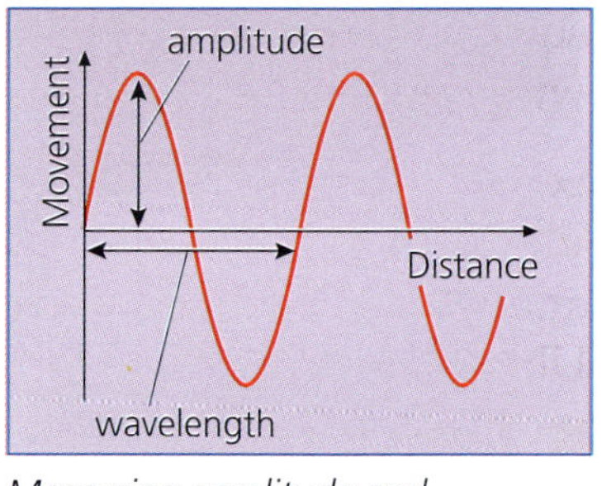

Measuring amplitude and wavelength in transverse waves

Electromagnetic waves such as light and radio waves are transverse waves – they all travel at the same speed in a vacuum.

Short wavelength, high-energy waves can be very damaging to people and other animals if they are absorbed by cells.

The table shows different groups of electromagnetic waves.

Wave group	Gamma rays	X-rays	Ultraviolet	Light	Infrared	Microwaves	Radio waves
Main use	Sterilising medical instruments and treating cancer	Looking inside the body and machines such as jet engines	Sun beds, fluorescent lamps and security marking	Seeing and photography	Remote controls and cooking such as grilling	Cooking and telephone and TV signals	Radio and TV broadcasting
Danger	Can cause cancer and damage to body cells and tissue	Can cause cancer and damage to body cells and tissue	Can cause skin cancer and damage to the eyes	Bright lights can damage the eyes	Causes skin burns	Causes heating of cells and tissue	None known

Electromagnetic waves are used to transmit information such as telephone calls, television and radio. These may be sent as either **analogue** or **digital** signals.

An analogue signal:

- is continually changing and can have any value up to the maximum value.

A digital signal:

- can only have certain values, usually 0 or 1;
- gives clearer reception as any unwanted noise is easily removed.

Both light and infrared waves are used to send information in digital form through an **optical fibre**. Because there is little energy loss in the optical fibre, these signals can travel long distances in optical fibres before they need to be amplified

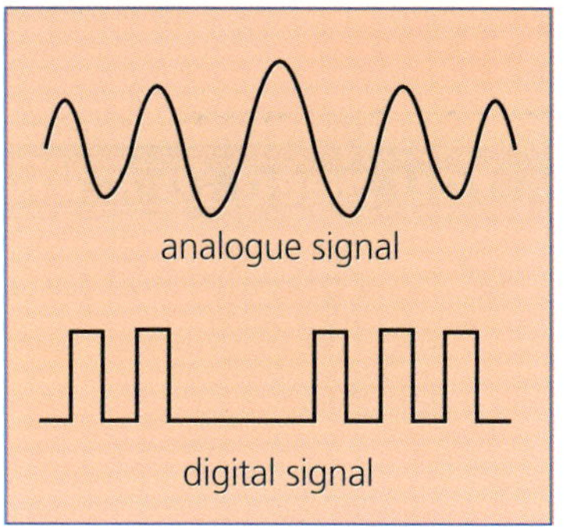

Analogue and digital signals

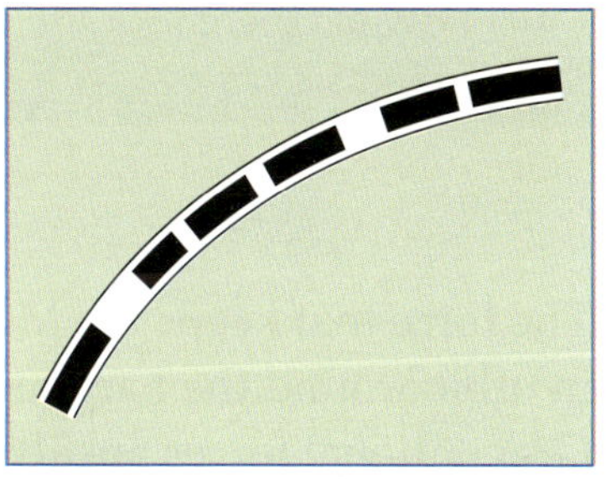

A digital signal travelling along an optical fibre

Light changing direction

Light and other electromagnetic waves normally travel in straight lines, but when they travel from one material into another their speed changes. This is known as **refraction** and it can cause a change in direction.

- When light travels from glass into air it slows down. It speeds up again as it leaves.
- Light travelling along a "normal" (a line drawn at right angles to the surface) does not change direction.

Sound is a longitudinal wave. It travels as a series of squashes and stretches. Human ears can detect sounds with frequencies in the range of 20 Hz to 20 000 Hz.

Sound waves with a frequency above 20 000 Hz are called **ultrasound**. Humans cannot hear ultrasound, although animals such as dogs and bats can detect some. Ultrasound is used to:

- produce computer images of the inside of the body – unlike X-rays, ultrasound does not damage cells and tissues so it is safe to use to examine a fetus, for example;
- explore the seabed and locate shipwrecks and shoals of fish.

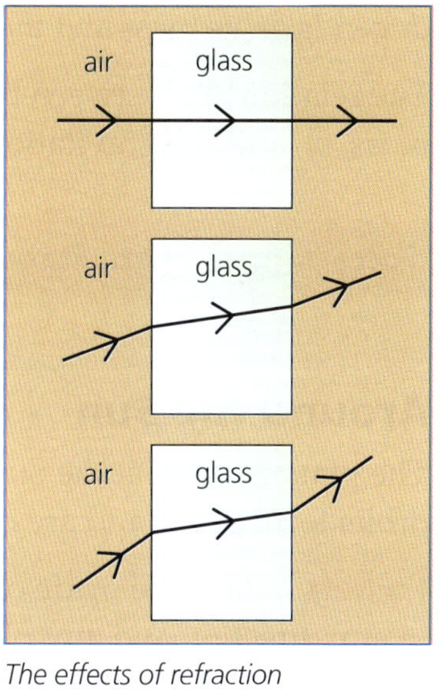

The effects of refraction

Questions

1. Which electromagnetic waves have the longest wavelength?
2. What always happens to a wave when it is refracted?
3. A ship sends a pulse of ultrasound to the seabed and detects the echo 0.84 s later. The speed of sound in water is 1500 m/s. How deep is the sea?
4. State one difference between sound and ultrasound.

Space

You need to know

- how gravitational forces affect the motion of planets, satellites and comets;
- that the Solar System is part of the Milky Way galaxy, which in turn is part of the Universe;
- how we search for life on other planets;
- what the 'Big Bang' theory of the origin of the Universe is and how to describe the life of a star;
- how the future of the Universe depends on the amount of mass present.

The force that keeps the Moon and artificial satellites in orbit around the Earth is a **gravitational force**. Gravitational forces are always attractive – they pull objects towards each other.

An artificial satellite is one that has been launched from Earth, for example a weather or communications satellite.

The size of the gravitational force acting on an object depends on its mass and the **gravitational field strength, *g***.

The relationship between the force on an object, *F*, its mass, *m*, and the gravitational field strength is:

Force = mass × gravitational field strength or $F = m \times g$

You need to be able to recall this relationship. It will not be given on exam or test papers.

Around the Sun

The planets all orbit the Sun in the same direction. Their orbits form a disc and are close to being circular.

Comets, which are made of ice and rock, can orbit the Sun in any direction and any plane. Their orbits are elliptical. The diagram shows the orbit of a comet and how the force on the comet changes during its orbit.

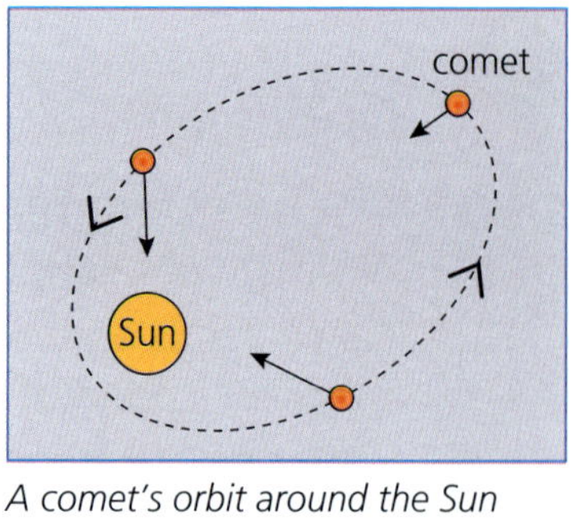

A comet's orbit around the Sun

Groups of millions of stars and their satellites that are held together by gravitational forces are called **galaxies**. The diagram on page 61 shows the **Milky Way** galaxy and the position of our Solar System.

The number of galaxies that make up the whole **Universe** is so vast that they cannot be counted.

Extraterrestrial

Many scientists believe that somewhere there must be a planet with conditions similar to those on Earth, where some form of life exists.

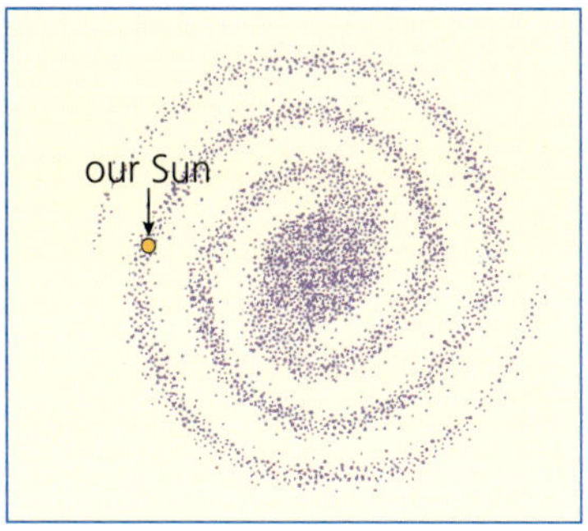

Ways of looking for life on other planets include:

- For near planets in our Solar System, such as Mars, we can send space probes to land on the planet. These probes carry out experiments on soil to search for evidence of primitive forms of life such as microbes.
- Scanning the radio wave spectrum to try to detect transmissions from more distant planets.

The stages in the life cycle of a small star like our Sun are:

- gravitational forces cause a cloud of dust and gas to collapse and become hot;
- when the temperature is high enough for nuclear fusion to start, a Sun is born;
- our Sun is in its **main sequence**, where the reaction that generates heat and light is the **fusion**, or joining together, of hydrogen nuclei to form helium nuclei;
- after its main sequence, our Sun will expand and cool to form a **red giant**;
- it will then contract and heat up again until it is a **white dwarf** and then cool to an invisible **black dwarf**.

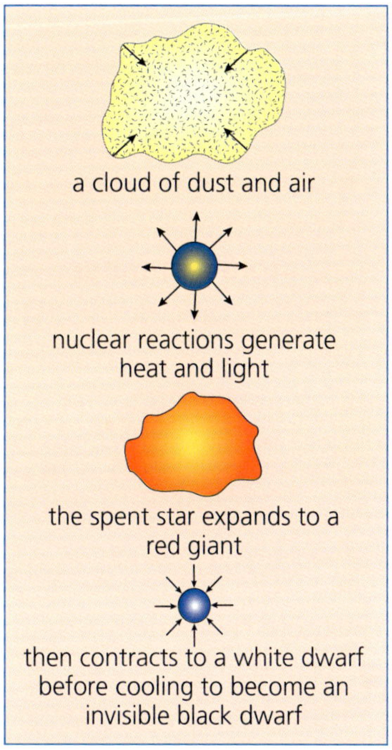

The stages in the life of a star

The Universe is thought to have begun with an enormous explosion, called the "**Big Bang**". The matter was created in this explosion, which has since formed into planets and stars. The Universe is known to be expanding. In the future it could:

- continue to expand if there is not enough mass for gravitational forces to halt this;
- reach and maintain a steady size;
- stop expanding and contract if there is enough mass for the gravitational forces to be strong enough.

Questions

1 What causes a star to begin to form in a dust cloud?

2 The Sun's pull on Jupiter is greater than the Sun's pull on the Earth, even though Jupiter is further away from the Sun. Suggest the reason for this.

3 State two ways in which the orbits of comets differ from those of planets.

Atoms

You need to know

- how to describe the atomic structure of an isotope from its symbol;
- how to describe alpha, beta and gamma radiation, their properties and some common uses;
- the meaning of background radiation and its sources;
- about the dangers of ionising radiation and the difficulties in disposing of radioactive waste.

The atomic nucleus contains two types of particle:

- Protons have a positive charge – the number of protons determines the element.
- Neutrons have the same mass as protons but are not charged. Atoms of the same element can have different numbers of neutrons.

The number of protons is the same as the position of the element in the periodic table.

Atoms are represented by a symbol that tells you about the structure of the nucleus. For example, the symbol for the most common form of carbon is $^{12}_{6}C$. The lower number, 6, is the **atomic number** and represents the number of protons in the nucleus. This identifies the element as carbon. The upper number is the total number of protons and neutrons (together called nucleons).

There are other forms of carbon, called **isotopes**. These include and $^{14}_{6}C$ and $^{11}_{6}C$.

Different isotopes of an element have the same number of protons but different numbers of neutrons. Work out the numbers of protons and neutrons in $^{14}_{6}C$ and $^{11}_{6}C$.

The nuclei of carbon-14, $^{14}_{6}C$, and carbon-11, $^{11}_{6}C$, are unstable. This means that:

- The nucleus can break down, giving out one or more radioactive emissions.
- A more stable nucleus of a different element is formed.

Properties of the three main types of radioactive emission are shown in the table.

It is not possible to completely absorb gamma radiation – its intensity can only be reduced.

Radioactive	Nature	Charge	Mass	Penetration
Alpha particle	Two neutrons and two protons	+2	4 × the mass of a proton	Absorbed by a sheet of paper or a few cm of air
Beta particle	Fast-moving electron	−1	1/2000 the mass of a proton	Absorbed by 3 mm of aluminium
Gamma ray	Short-wavelength electromagnetic radiation	0	0	Intensity is reduced by several cm of lead

Some common uses of radioactivity include:

- Alpha particles are used in smoke alarms – the smoke absorbs the alpha particles so they cannot ionise the air.
- Beta particles are used to control the thickness of sheet materials such as aluminium foil.
- Gamma rays are used to sterilise food and medical instruments.

Gamma rays are used for sterilising because they kill microbes.

We live in a radioactive world – we are constantly being bombarded with radiation that is called **background radiation**. The chart shows the sources of background radiation in the UK.

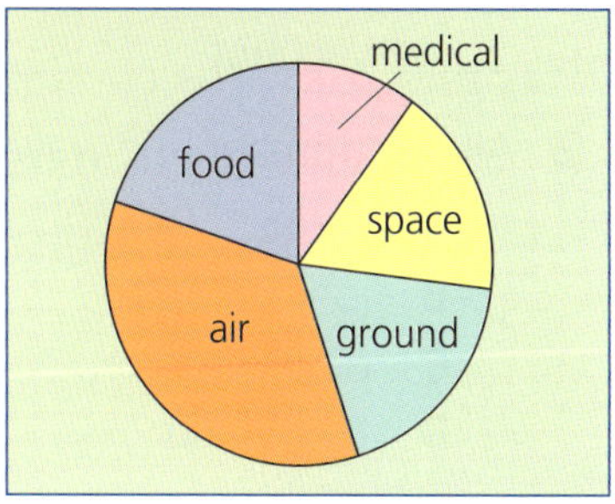

Exposure to radiation can be damaging to humans. It can:

- cause mutations – changes to the DNA of sex cells can result in the birth of deformed offspring;
- damage cells and tissue, which results in cancer.

Because of this, we need to take care when disposing of radioactive waste from hospitals and nuclear power stations.

Radioactive waste can emit harmful radiation for thousands of years. It needs to be placed in sites where the radiation cannot reach and damage people. Burying it underground is one possibility but there are problems with doing this:

- There could be changes in the geology that may expose the material or cause the containers to crack.
- Radioactive material could enter the water supply.
- The waste needs to be buried in very deep chambers so that the emissions are absorbed by the ground.
- There is a danger of making the soil radioactive.

The problems of disposing of radioactive waste have resulted in a decline in the number of nuclear power stations in the UK over recent years.

Questions

1 Describe the nuclear structure of $^{15}_{8}O$.

2 Oxygen-15 and oxygen-16 are isotopes of oxygen. In what way are they the same and in what way are they different?

3 Smoke alarms use sources of alpha radiation. Explain why these sources are not harmful to people in the same room.

Practice module test

You will have 20 minutes to answer these questions

1 Radio waves, light and X-rays all:

- **A** have the same frequency
- **B** have the same amplitude
- **C** have the same wavelength
- **D** travel at the same speed in a vacuum

2 All electromagnetic waves are:

- **A** acute
- **B** longitudinal
- **C** obtuse
- **D** transverse

3 Which waves are used for cooking food?

- **A** microwaves and X-rays
- **B** X-rays and gamma rays
- **C** microwaves and infrared waves
- **D** gamma rays and infrared waves

4 Sound is a:

- **A** longitudinal wave
- **B** radio wave
- **C** television wave
- **D** transverse wave

5 X-rays are used to:

- **A** broadcast television programmes
- **B** broadcast radio programmes
- **C** cook food
- **D** examine bones for fractures

6 Which arrow in the diagram shows the direction of the Earth's pull on the Moon?

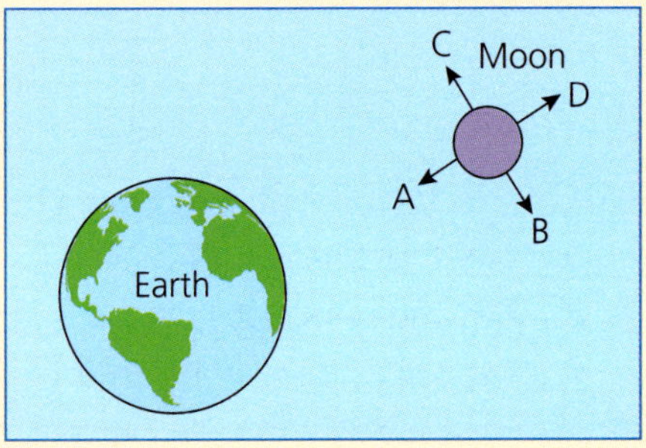

7 A galaxy is a collection of:

- **A** comets
- **B** planets
- **C** satellites
- **D** stars

8 A star:

- **A** orbits a moon
- **B** orbits a planet
- **C** can be seen by the light it emits
- **D** can be seen by the light it reflects

9 The orbit of a comet is in the shape of a:

- **A** circle
- **B** ellipse
- **C** oblong
- **D** square

10 The number of protons in an atom of ${}^{14}_{7}N$ is:

- **A** 2
- **B** 7
- **C** 14
- **D** 21

11 Compared to ${}^{1}_{1}H$, ${}^{2}_{1}H$ has:

- **A** more electrons
- **B** more neutrons
- **C** more nuclei
- **D** more protons

12 The most penetrative type of radioactive emission is:

- **A** alpha
- **B** beta
- **C** gamma
- **D** delta

13 The frequency of a wave is:

- **A** the time taken to complete one cycle
- **B** the length of one cycle
- **C** the number of waves that occur each day
- **D** the number of waves that occur each second

14 In the visible spectrum, the colour that has the longest wavelength is:

- **A** red
- **B** orange
- **C** green
- **D** blue

15 When light is refracted changes occur to its:

- **A** speed and wavelength
- **B** speed and frequency
- **C** frequency and direction
- **D** frequency and wavelength

16 Fluorescent lamps emit:

- **A** X-rays
- **B** gamma rays
- **C** ultraviolet radiation
- **D** radio waves

17 Light slows down as it travels from air into glass. This is known as:

- **A** deflection
- **B** diffraction
- **C** reflection
- **D** refraction

18 A moon is:

- **A** a planet
- **B** a satellite of a planet
- **C** a satellite of a star
- **D** the centre of a solar system

19 ${}^{14}_{6}C$ has:

- **A** 6 neutrons in its nucleus
- **B** 14 neutrons in its nucleus
- **C** 6 protons in its nucleus
- **D** 14 neutrons in its nucleus

20 The gravitational field strength at the surface of the Earth is 10 N/kg.
That at the surface of Jupiter is 24 N/kg.
A person weighs 600 N on Earth. The person's weight on Jupiter would be:

- **A** 60 kg
- **B** 1440 kg
- **C** 60 N
- **D** 1440 N

21 Gravitational forces:

- **A** only act between objects that are charged
- **B** only act between objects that are magnetic
- **C** are always attractive
- **D** are always repulsive

22 The orbits of comets:

- **A** are circular
- **B** are elliptical
- **C** are always in the same plane
- **D** are always in the same direction

23 The nucleus of an atom represented by the symbol ${}^{23}_{11}Na$ has:

- **A** 11 protons
- **B** 12 protons
- **C** 11 nucleons
- **D** 12 nucleons

24 Of the three main types of radioactive emission, alpha radiation:

- **A** has the smallest charge
- **B** has the smallest mass
- **C** has the lowest penetration
- **D** causes the least ionisation

Answers to these questions can be found on pages 140–144

Getting it right

(a) The table shows the groups of waves that make up the electromagnetic spectrum.

Gamma rays	X-rays	Ultraviolet	Light		Microwaves	Radio

(i) Which group of waves is missing from the table?

Infrared **[1]**

(ii) Which group of waves shown in the table is used for cooking food?

Microwaves **[1]**

(iii) Which group of waves shown in the table is used to send data along optical fibres?

Light **[1]**

(iv) Going through the spectrum from gamma rays to radio waves, how do the wavelengths and frequencies change?

The wavelengths increase and the frequencies decrease. **[2]**

You need to know how the different groups of waves fit into the electromagnetic spectrum.

Infrared waves are also used to cook food and transmit data along optical fibres, but they are not shown in the table.

(b) The diagram shows an ultrasound scan of a fetus.

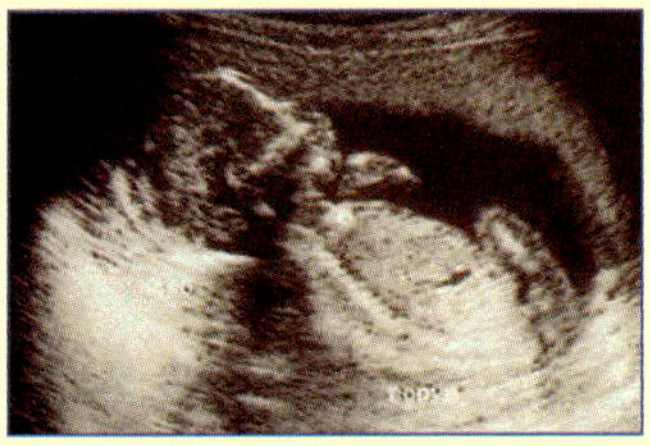

(i) Why is ultrasound preferred to X-rays for viewing a fetus?

Ultrasound is safe to use because it does not damage cells and tissues but X-rays do. **[2]**

(ii) How is an ultrasound scan produced?

Pulses of ultrasound are emitted by a probe. The ultrasound is reflected by the fetus and these reflections are detected by the probe. A computer uses the information from the probe to build up a picture.

[3]

Remember, this question is about the science of an ultrasound scan, so answers such as "the patient lies on a table…" would not be awarded any marks.

Food production and the environment

All life depends on a supply of energy. Energy must enter and flow through an ecosystem for a range of organisms to survive.

The first topic in this module is about a key group of organisms that allow energy input into an ecosystem – the green plants.

Energy passes through an ecosystem via food chains and webs. This is the subject of the second topic. The diversity of organisms and their relationships in different ecosystems is outlined in the third topic.

Living organisms produce waste and finally die. The fourth topic explains the role of microorganisms in recycling.

Humans live throughout the ecosystems of the world and need nutrients to survive. The fifth topic is about how we achieve the maximum production of human food.

Control of plant activity

You need to know

- how plant cells differ from animal cells;
- an outline of photosynthesis and the key factors that affect the process;
- about the distribution and uses of sugars in plants;
- about the absorption and transport of water and minerals in plants;
- the role of guard cells in controlling water loss through transpiration;
- the role of plant hormones in controlling plant growth;
- commercial uses of plant hormones.

How do plant and animal cells differ?

The diagrams below show typical plant and animal cells.

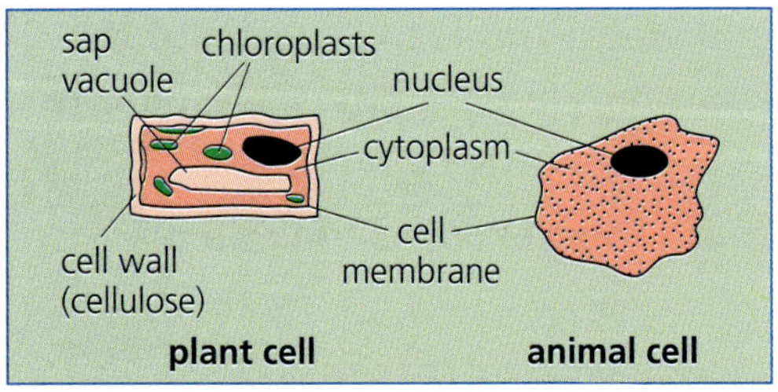

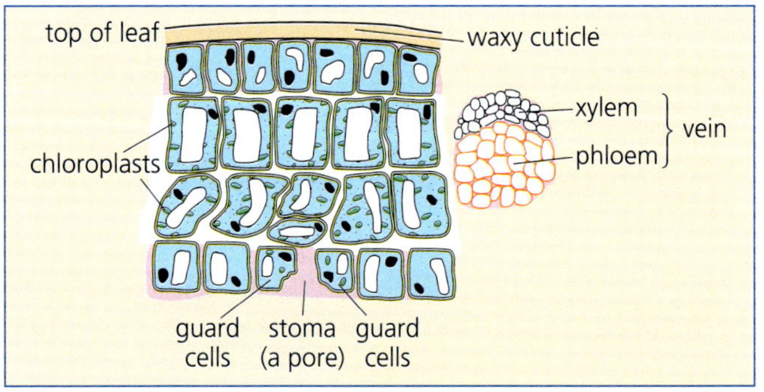

Cells with **chloroplasts** are found in various parts of plant shoots but there are more in the leaves. The section through a leaf in the diagram above shows three types of cell with chloroplasts.

There are more chloroplasts in the upper part of leaves, to absorb maximum light. The chloroplasts contain **chlorophyll**, a vital substance in the process of **photosynthesis**. Water for the process is stored in the vacuoles. The veins form a tubular transport system.

Learn the word equation for photosynthesis – you may be asked to complete it in an exam. Do not write chlorophyll along the equation line. Keep to the ingredients and products shown.

Photosynthesis traps light energy in glucose molecules, but it is **respiration** that releases it.

Photosynthesis

Green plants have the ability to harness light energy using photosynthesis.

Photosynthesis produces

- glucose, which contains energy (trapped as chemical energy)
- Oxygen is also produced, as a waste product.

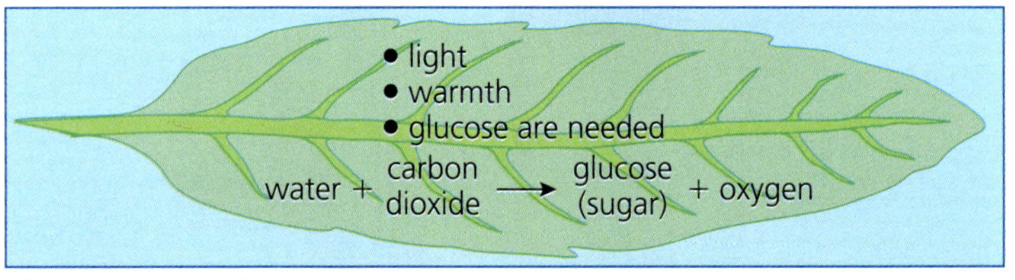

The process of photosynthesis

Plants need mineral salts

Plants also need mineral salts for healthy growth. The roots absorb mineral salts.

Mineral	Used to make	Affects
nitrate	protein	growth
magnesium ions	chlorophyl	photosynthesis

How do plants take in water?

Roots absorb water through root hairs – cells with special adaptations to absorb water as well as minerals. Each root hair is a long thin cell that projects into the soil. Water is taken into a plant by the process of **osmosis**.

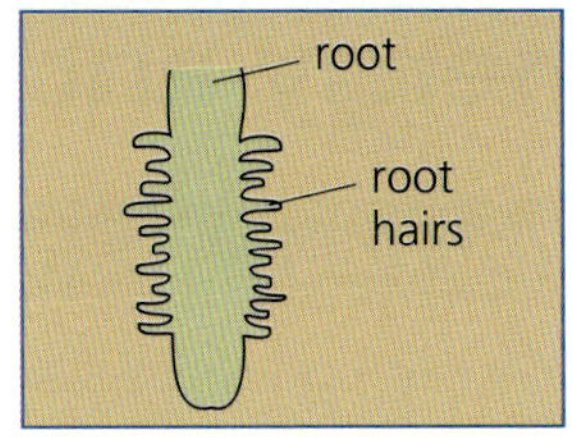

Diffusion

When a spoonful of sugar is put into a cup of tea the sugar molecules move so that they are in equal concentration everywhere, even without stirring. Molecules in fluids and gases move from an area of high concentration to where they are in low concentration. This is **diffusion**.

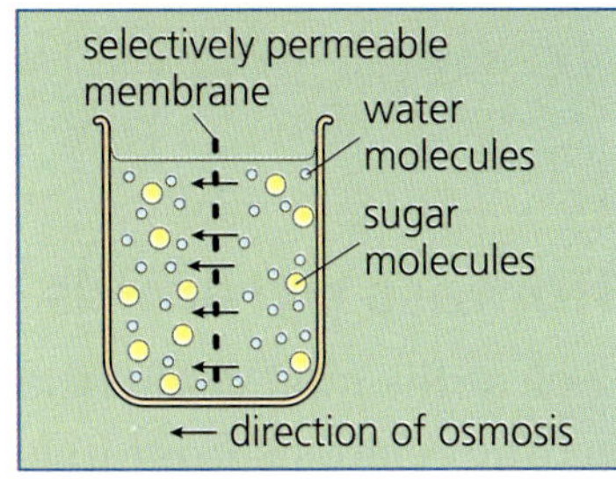

The process of osmosis

Osmosis

This is a special type of diffusion that takes place when a solution of higher concentration is separated from a solution of lower concentration by a **selectively permeable membrane**. This has tiny holes that only allow water molecules to pass through. The water molecules move from the less concentrated solution to the more concentrated solution. The process depends on the concentration of solutions inside and outside the cells.

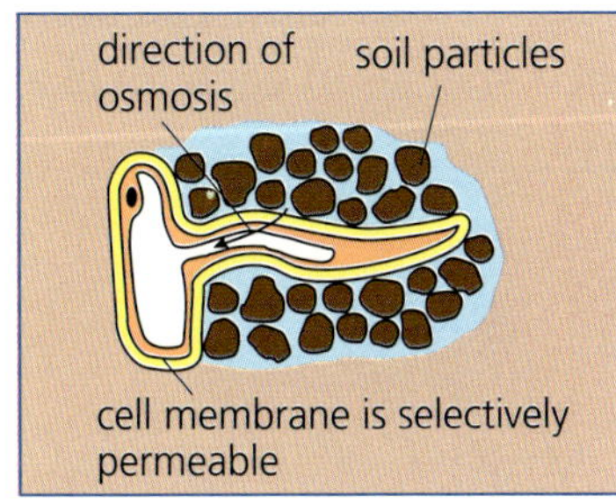

Absorption of water by a root hair – water moves into the root hair until the concentration of water molecules in the sap vacuole is equal to the concentration of water around the soil particles

Water transport in plants

Once inside a plant, water is transported to all cells. Across a root, water goes from cell to cell by osmosis. Water reaches the middle of a root and enters tube-like vessels known as the **xylem**. These vessels consist of dead hollow cells. Each cell is joined to the next to form a long tube, ideal for water transport. A plant needs water:

- for photosynthesis, where it is used with carbon dioxide to make glucose;
- for all enzyme-based reactions;
- to give its cells hydrostatic strength, known as **turgidity**.

Plants lose water by the process of **transpiration**. Water vapour diffuses through pores in the leaf, called **stomata**. Water evaporates from many surfaces of a plant, but much more is lost by the stomata. Open stomata allow more water loss. Stomata can open and close in response to different conditions. Most plants close their stomata at night.

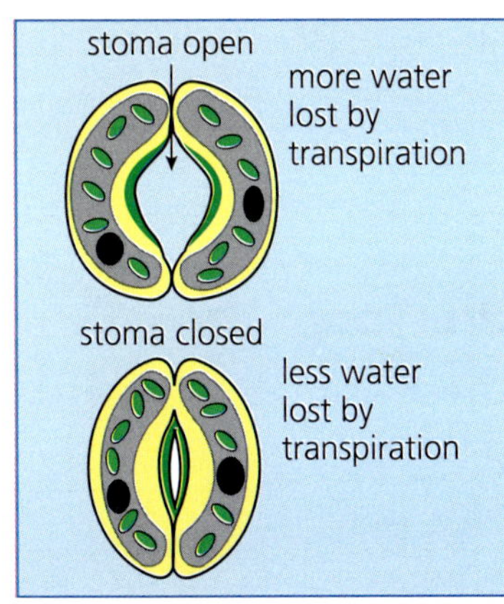

Questions

1. Which tissue transports (a) water, (b) glucose through a plant?
2. What is osmosis?
3. Which cells control transpiration?

Energy and ecosystems

You need to know

- that food chains can be represented quantitatively by biomass pyramids;
- how energy is passed through an ecosystem;
- how energy is lost along a food chain;
- that mammals have problems with heat loss.

Biomass pyramids

Look at the food chain below. The arrows show the feeding relationships but give no indication of numbers or size of the organisms. Biomass can be measured and is the mass of a species. The biomass pyramid is the total mass of each species at each level along a food chain.

Remember to put the arrows in the right direction in exam questions.

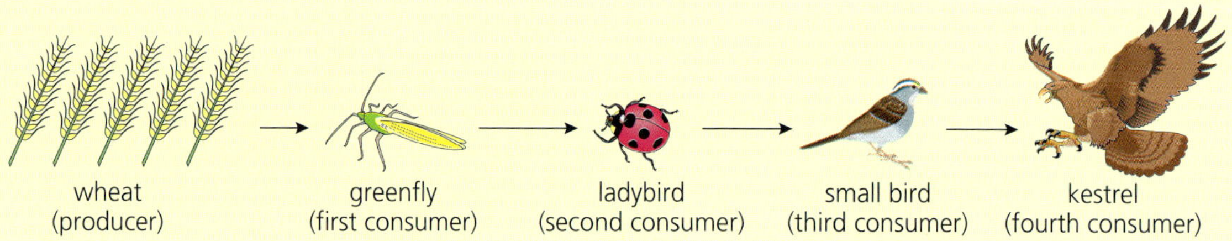

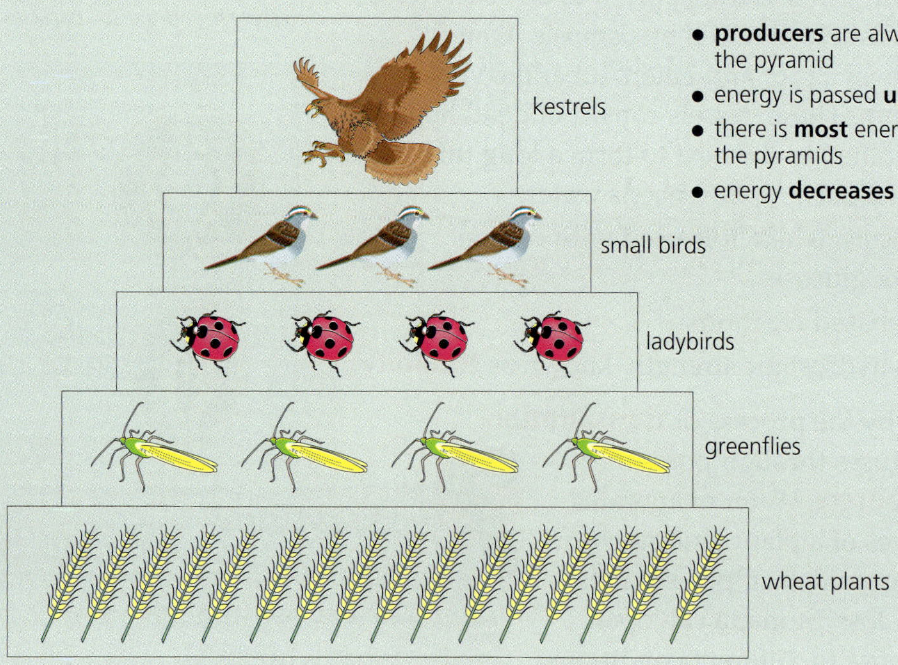

- **producers** are always the base of the pyramid
- energy is passed **up** the pyramid
- there is **most** energy at the base of the pyramids
- energy **decreases** up the pyramid

A biomass pyramid

Energy flow through an ecosystem

Food chains interlink through food webs in an ecosystem. Energy enters an ecosystem via producers. Each species at each level is a food source for the next consumer – right up to the top consumer. Energy is lost throughout a food chain. The next level of organisms always has less available energy than the previous one.

Warm-blooded animals need a lot of energy to maintain their body heat. Mammals lose a lot of heat energy to the air.

Energy is lost along a food chain because:

- respiration releases heat energy so it is not available for the next level;
- organisms excrete substances, e.g. sweat and urine, which loses energy.

This is why flies follow us when we sweat – the sweat contains nutrients.

Natural ecosystems

An ecosystem consists of:

- an area that has particular characteristics, such as desert;
- a number of organisms living together in a community;
- the abiotic factors of the environment, such as the water content of the soil;
- a stable environment where substances are recycled, helping to maintain the community.

Biodiversity

Even a desert ecosystem supports a wide range of different living things. This is known as **biodiversity**. Rainforest has even greater biodiversity because of the greater energy input into this ecosystem. Each type of organism contributes to the success of the ecosystem. Producers allow the energy flow in and decomposers recycle nutrients from waste products and dead organisms.

Biodiversity means different species in an area.

Questions

1. What type of organism is at the start of all food chains?
2. How is energy lost along a food chain?
3. Only one species of tree is planted in a forest. What effect will this have on biodiversity?
4. Explain the effects of weeds on the amount of wheat produced in a field.

Action of microorganisms in ecosystems

You need to know

- ✔ about the process of decay;
- ✔ the carbon and nitrogen cycles;
- ✔ the effects of deforestation;
- ✔ the importance of conservation.

Decomposers and the compost heap

Material such as leaves and animal faeces are put in a heap. Decomposing bacteria and fungi begin to rot down the material by secreting enzymes that break down the organic material. They breed in large numbers in the heap. The heap gets smaller and is full of minerals, so is useful as a fertiliser for plants.

Some garden centres sell packets of bacteria as a starter for compost heaps. However, they are not really necessary – bacteria are in the air, water and soil all around us.

After several days, decomposers such as bacteria become established and increase in numbers as they reproduce. Decay speeds up and the heap may steam. This is caused by the heat energy released during respiration of the microorganisms.

Requirements for decay	How does this help decay?
presence of decomposer bacteria and fungi	if there were no microorganisms then there would not be any decay!
oxygen	many decomposers respire aerobically
moisture	needed if the enzymes produced by the decomposers are to work
suitable temperature	needed if the enzymes produced by the decomposers are to work

The carbon cycle

The air contains about 0.03% carbon dioxide. The amount is kept in balance by the processes involved in the carbon cycle. There are three key processes in the carbon cycle:

- Photosynthesis, which removes carbon dioxide from the air, fixing it in carbohydrate molecules.
- Respiration, which breaks down organic compounds, releasing carbon dioxide back into the air.
- Combustion, which also releases the carbon dioxide back into the air.

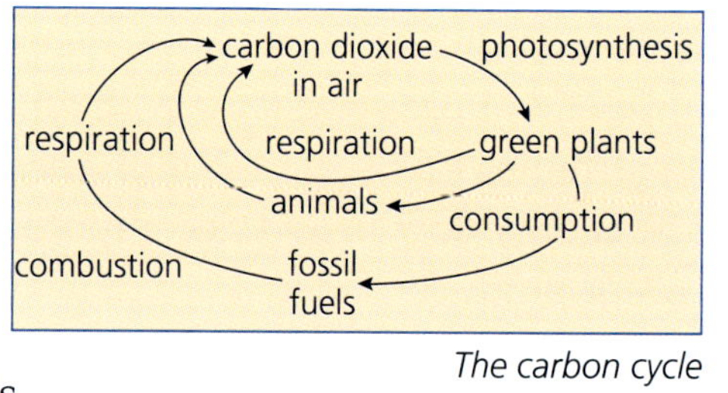

The carbon cycle

Deforestation

The human population of the world continues to increase. This means that we need more areas for houses, factories and farming and has led to deforestation – the cutting down of large areas of trees. There are several disadvantages to deforestation, including:

Too much burning and not enough photosynthesis? It is important that processes remain in balance. Cutting down the rainforests is not a good idea. Conservation means that we should keep these habitats.

- it reduces the amount of oxygen produced by photosynthesis;
- it destroys the habitats and food sources of many organisms;
- tree roots are no longer able to bind the soil, leading to soil erosion and land slip;
- it increases levels of carbon dioxide in the air, leading to global warming.

The nitrogen cycle

The element nitrogen is needed in all amino acids and, therefore, proteins. This nitrogen is of no direct use to most organisms but it can be converted into a useful form during the nitrogen cycle.

Nitrate fertilisers – supply plants with the element nitrogen in a suitable form to make amino acids, then proteins.

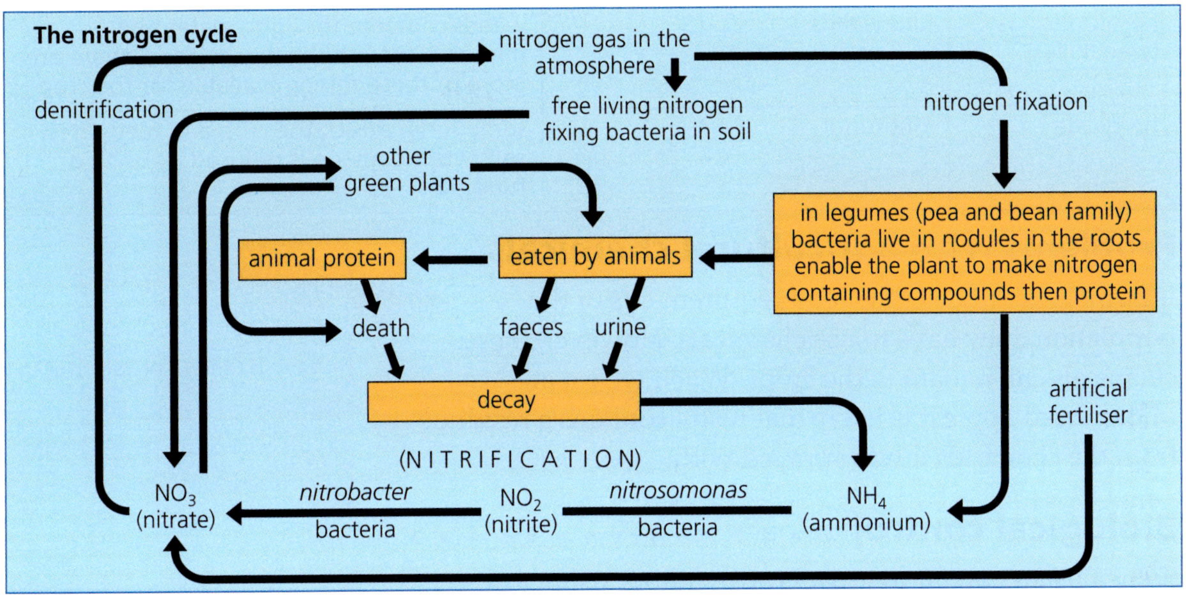

The nitrogen cycle

Questions

1. What are the optimum conditions for decay?
2. Why is it necessary for materials to be decomposed?
3. Why is a compost heap turned over halfway through the decay process?
4. State the three main processes in the carbon cycle.
5. Give reasons for deforestation.
6. What is nitrogen fixation?

Maximising food production

You need to know

- how we use a range of chemicals to achieve a high crop yield;
- about the dangers of overusing pesticides;
- how we use biological control in crop production.

Using chemicals to increase crop yields

Fertilisers provide plant nutrients important for healthy growth. A crop can also be given other chemicals that can result in a maximum yield. The table below shows the effect of each chemical.

Selective herbicides kill the weeds but not the crop.

Type of chemical	What is its effect?	How does it help achieve a high yield?
pesticide	kills pests like greenfly and mice	reduces damage to crop by the pest
insecticide	kills insect pests like greenfly	reduces damage to crop by the insect pest
herbicide (weedkiller)	kills weeds	weeds compete for light, water and minerals, so with the weeds gone, there are more of these things available for the crop
fungicide	kills fungi	some fungi attack the crop and feed on its cells – this damage is reduced by using a fungicide

Problems with agricultural chemicals

If farmers are to meet the food requirements of the population, they have to use chemicals. However, these chemicals can remain in the crops. When we eat an undamaged apple it is likely that it still contains a residue from the chemicals it was sprayed with.

Pesticide is a general term given to chemicals used to kill animals that damage crops. For example slug pellets kill slugs and snails.

Biological control

Some farmers prefer to grow crops without using any man-made chemicals, but they still use natural chemicals. This is known as **organic farming**.

There are several variations of this method, including using a predator to kill a pest (prey). For example, predatory wasps are used to kill greenhouse whitefly.

Crops such as tomatoes are attacked by a sap-sucking insect, the whitefly. Whitefly females lay eggs on tomato leaves. Larvae hatch from the eggs. A predatory female wasp lays an egg into a whitefly larva. Days later an adult wasp emerges from the larva. The wasp has used the larva as a food source and only its outer shell is left.

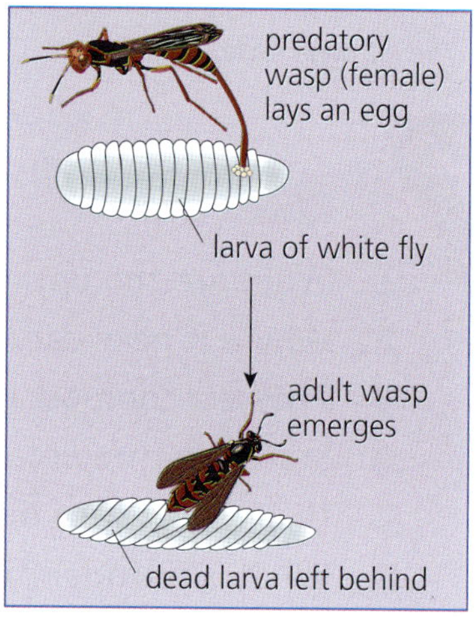

The wasps breed quickly – a big advantage. An insecticide usually needs several applications, but this method of control needs just one introduction at the beginning – nature does the rest.

Another method of biological control is the release of sterile males. This method relies on the fact that some insects mate only once. For example, the New World screw fly attacks farm animals (and people) in some countries. It lays eggs in cuts and the larvae attack the body internally. Eventually it can kill the victim. The answer has been to subject adult flies to a dose of radiation. This causes every male to become sterile. Released in large numbers from aeroplanes, into problem areas each sterile male mates with a local female. She lays sterile eggs that never hatch out, and the population is reduced.

Note that you never use the predator method of biological control **and** a pesticide. The predators may be killed by the chemical.

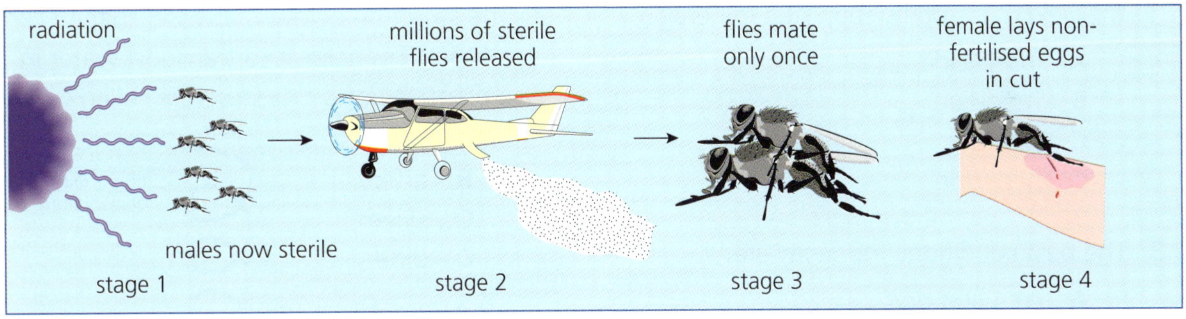

Greenhouse management

In warm countries greenhouses are not necessary. In the UK, there are cold months when frosts can kill many plants, so greenhouses are used as a controlled environment.

Growing plants in greenhouses is known as **intensive farming**. The aim is to provide optimum conditions for the growing crop. Large commercial greenhouses are used to supply supermarkets. Large amounts of the crop can be transported at the same time, which reduces costs. It is important in intensive crop production that costs must be justified. Profits need to be maximised.

A greenhouse gives improved conditions with a **higher temperature**. Plants can take advantage of the light for **photosynthesis**.

Questions

1. How do pesticides help farmers to produce high crop yields?
2. A wheat field is full of weeds. What would using a selective herbicide achieve?
3. What name is given to fruits and vegetables produced without using man-made chemicals
4. What can be used instead of chemicals to kill crop pests.

Practice module test

You will have 17 minutes to answer these questions

1 Which diagram below shows the biomass pyramid for the food chain?
pondweed → tadpole → dragonfly → bird

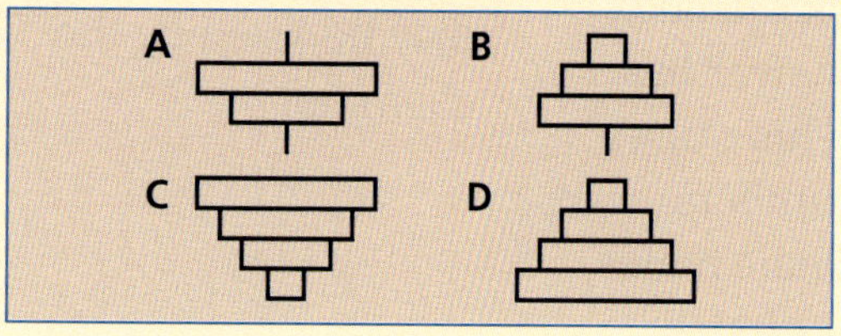

2 Which of the following chemicals increases the yield of a crop by supplying minerals?

A insecticide
B fungicide
C fertiliser
D herbicide

3 The best conditions for decay are:

A cold and dry
B cold and wet
C warm and dry
D warm and damp

4 The diagram below shows a plant palisade cell. Which of the items labelled (**A**, **B**, **C** or **D**) is not found in an animal cell?

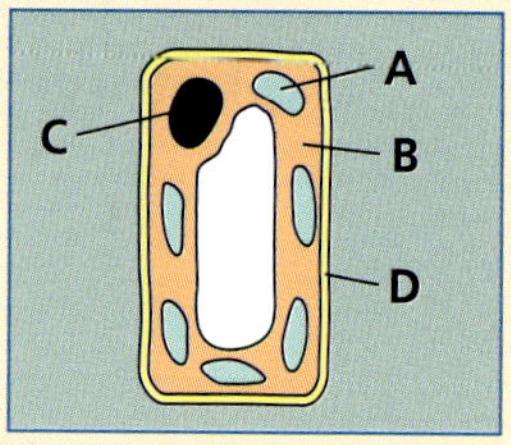

5 Which two words are needed to complete the following word equation for photosynthesis:

________ + ________ = glucose + oxygen

A water and carbon dioxide
B water and sugar
C carbon dioxide and sugar
D water and oxygen

6 The diagram below shows a plant that has lost mass because of water loss. The process shown by the change in mass is:

A growth
B photosynthesis
C transpiration
D perspiration

7 The structure below is a vessel shaped like a tube. This helps it to transport water in a plant. What is this structure called?

A phloem
B artery
C xylem
D pipe

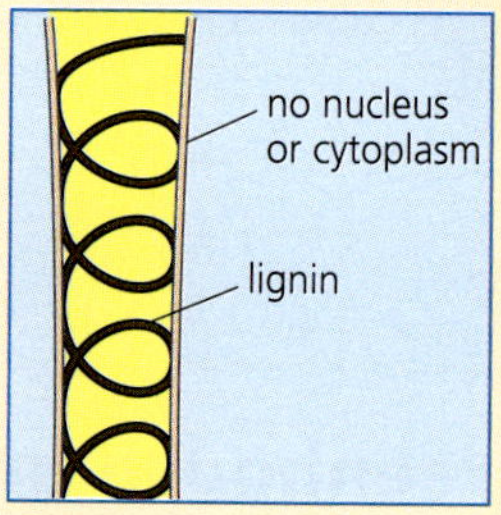

8 In a compost heap containing leaves, after three months there will be:

A more leaves
B more bacteria
C less bacteria
D more proteins

9 Combustion of fossil fuels releases water and:

A sulphur
B nitrogen
C carbon dioxide
D oxygen

10 A herbicide is a type of chemical that:

A is a nutrient needed by a plant to grow
B kills weeds
C kills pests
D kills fungi

11 The diagram below shows a Visking tubing bag used to demonstrate osmosis. The bag containing sugar solution of higher concentration was placed in another sugar solution of lower concentration. The bag increased in mass because:

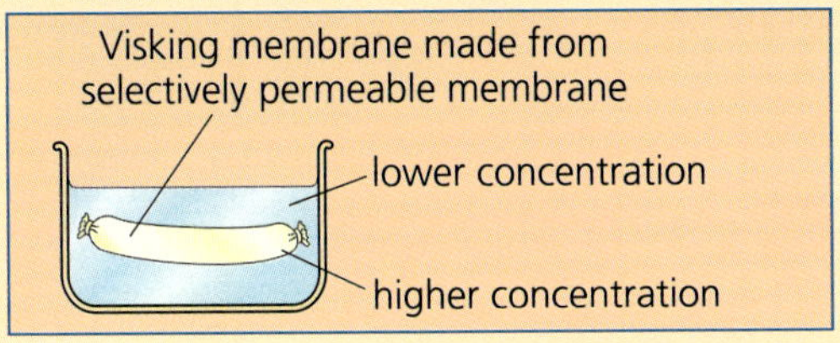

- **A** sugar molecules entered the bag
- **B** water molecules entered the bag
- **C** sugar solution entered the bag
- **D** water molecules left the bag

12 Pots X and Y each contained a wheat plant and a weed. Pot X was sprayed with a selective herbicide. Pot Y was not. The diagrams show the plants before spraying and a week after spraying. The wheat grew very well because:

- **A** the weed was killed, providing more minerals for the wheat
- **B** the selective herbicide supplied more nutrients to the wheat
- **C** the wheat received more water than the weed
- **D** the wheat received more light than the weed

13 Vaseline makes a surface waterproof. Equal masses of leaves of the same plant species were treated with Vaseline in different ways. They were left in the same conditions.
Group 1 – Vaseline on upper surface
Group 2 – Vaseline on lower surface
Group 3 – Vaseline on upper and lower surfaces
The leaves were weighed at the start and after 2 weeks. Beginning with the greatest first, the correct order of mass would be:

- **A** 1 2 3
- **B** 3 2 1
- **C** 3 1 2
- **D** 2 1 3

14 The diagram below shows a test tube containing some water and pondweed. The tube was given a supply of light. Which statement correctly describes what is taking place in the tube?

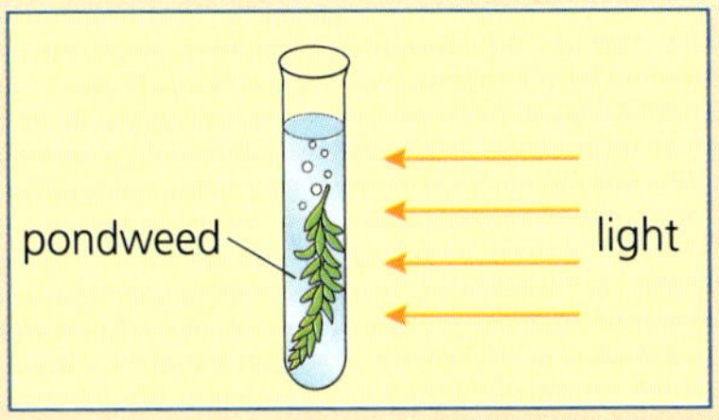

- **A** just respiration would take place
- **B** just photosynthesis would take place
- **C** both respiration and photosynthesis take place
- **D** transpiration and photosynthesis are taking place

15 Which of the following describes the loss of energy from the food chain?
rose bush → greenfly → ladybird

- **A** photosynthesis
- **B** respiration
- **C** greenfly are eaten by a ladybird
- **D** a rose bush is attacked by greenfly

16 Which one of the following is reduced as a result of deforestation?

- **A** oxygen content in the air
- **B** carbon dioxide in the air
- **C** nitrogen content of the air
- **D** the chances of soil erosion

Answers to these questions can be found on pages 140–144

Getting it right

1 The flow diagram below shows the nitrogen cycle.

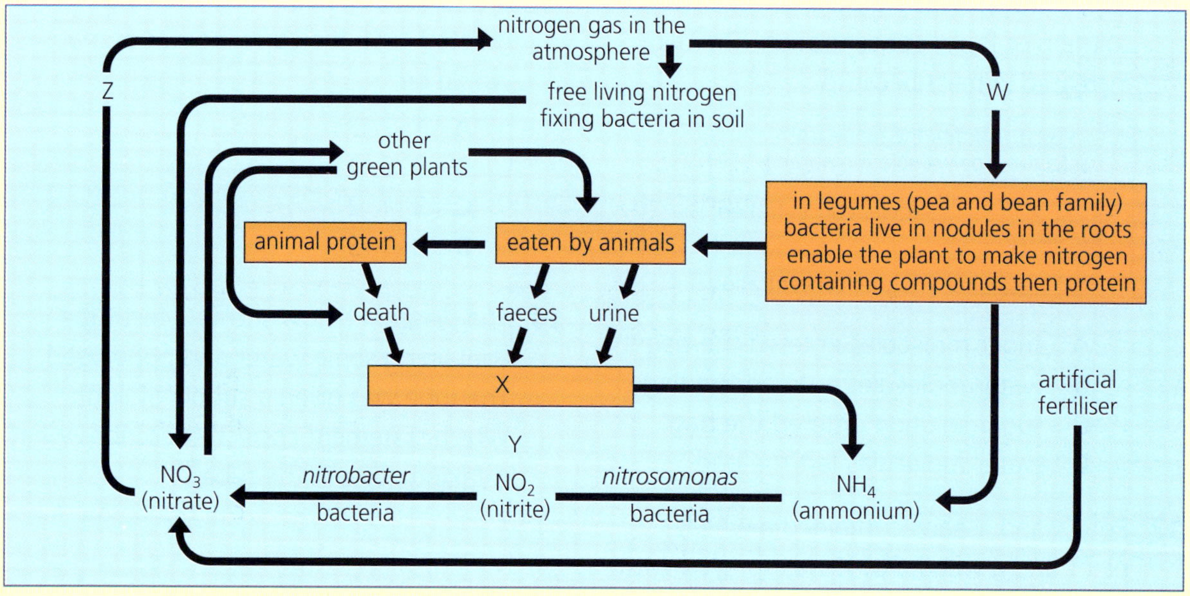

(a) (i) Listed below are processes from the nitrogen cycle:

nitrification   denitrification   nitrogen fixation   decay

Link each process, W, X, Y and Z to the list above

W = nitrogen fixation; X = decay;
Y = nitrification; Z = denitrification **[4]**

The list given should be a cue to your memory.

(ii) An animal dies. What happens to the energy contained in the organism during decay?

Decomposer microorganisms
break animal tissue down using enzymes
absorb nutrients
respire
release energy **[4]**

Take care here. Candidates often indicate that the energy of decay 'goes into the ground'. This is wrong – energy is released, which fuels the life of microorganisms.

(iii) Why are nitrate fertilisers used in crop fields?

Promote crop growth (increase yield),
so growth not held back by
deficiencies; help plants make proteins. **[2]**

(b) Why are magnesium ions needed by a plant?

Used in chlorophyll molecule. **[1]**

Look carefully at the specification – it gives you the information needed. Magnesium ions are used for chlorophyll so help photosynthesis.

Health and exercise

Our lifestyle can either enhance or harm our health. This module covers some of the body's major systems and associated health issues.

The first topic in the module is about the structure and function of the respiratory system and the problems associated with smoking tobacco.

Chemicals such as nutrients and hormones are transported around the body. The second topic covers the structure and functions of the circulatory system and associated health problems.

Energy released inside our cells gives us life. The third topic explains how respiration releases energy and how we can maintain our health by exercising.

Finally, two important health problems are explained – drug misuse and inherited disease.

The lungs

You need to know

- ✔ about the structure and function of the human respiratory system;
- ✔ about the process of ventilation (breathing in and breathing out);
- ✔ details of the respiratory diseases caused by smoking tobacco.

The human respiratory system

The complex structures of the human respiratory system have two functions:

- to supply the blood with oxygen;
- to remove toxic carbon dioxide from the blood.

The diagram below shows the human **thorax**, the name for the chest area. The continuous action of breathing in and out is known as **ventilation**.

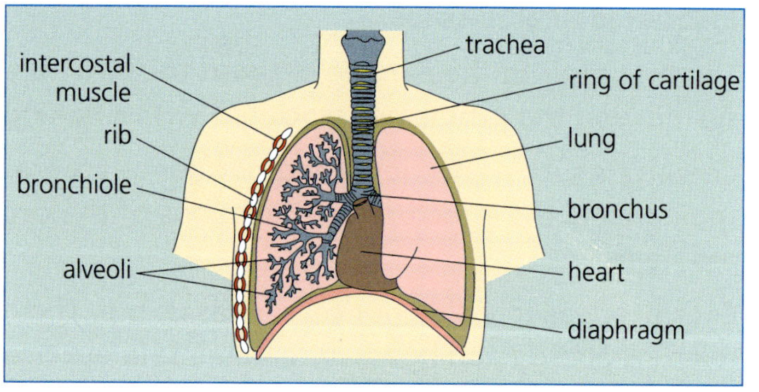

The human thorax

You will often need to explain how the structures of the respiratory system work together during breathing in and breathing out.

The table below explains the structure and function of the various parts of the human respiratory system.

Structure	Function
bronchus	transports air, connects trachea to bronchioles
bronchioles	connect bronchi to alveoli
alveoli	one cell thick, large surface area, covered by capillaries, oxygen diffuses into blood and carbon dioxide out of blood
diaphragm	a band of muscle that can make air pressure in the lungs lower or higher than that outside body
ribs	protect lungs and heart, help to lift or lower chest
intercostal muscles	can lift chest upwards and outwards or downwards and inwards lungs

As we breathe in:

- the diaphragm contracts and flattens;
- the intercostal muscles contract, causing the rib cage to move upwards and outwards;
- this creates a lower pressure in the lungs than in the air outside, so air flows in through the nose/mouth, down the trachea into the lungs.

Learn this sequence carefully – it is likely to be worth 6 marks in an exam!

Clean air

The environment inside the nose cavity is moist and warm. Goblet cells in the membranes produce a fluid – **mucus**. The mucus traps dust particles and bacteria. The cilia move the mucus to the back of the throat, where the "dirty" mucus is swallowed, or coughed up.

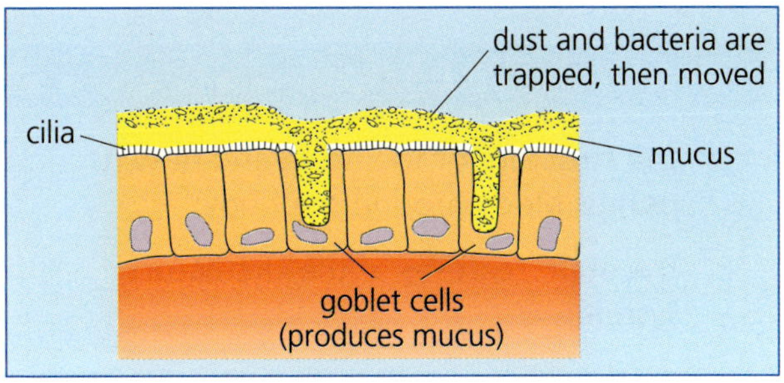

Smoking can seriously damage your health

Smoking tobacco – cigarettes in particular is dangerous. There are so many risks associated with tobacco that health deterioration is a certainty.

The diagram shows the surface of an alveoli. It is covered with **tar**.

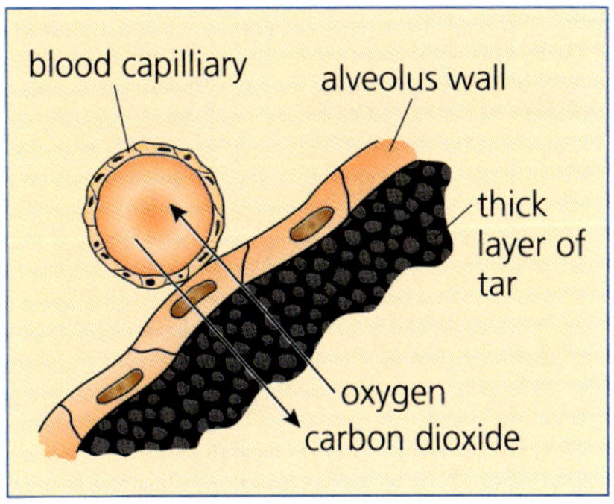

Smoking causes serious diseases.

Cancer

- Tar released by burning cigarettes contains substances that cause cancer (**carcinogens**).
- Carcinogens can affect the DNA in cells.
- Normal cells in the lungs can change into cancer cells.
- Cancer cells grow quickly and are abnormal, preventing many organs from working properly.

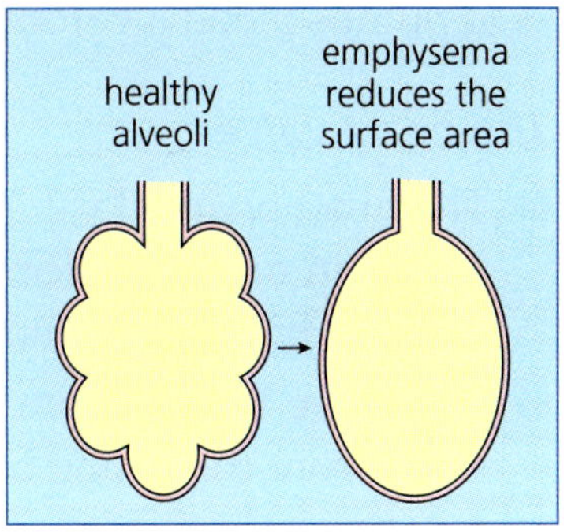

Emphysema

- The alveoli walls become less elastic.
- This results in a much smaller surface area for the exchange of oxygen and carbon dioxide.

Fighting the addiction

The nicotine in cigarettes is highly addictive. Giving up needs determination. To support someone trying to give up there are nicotine patches and nicotine gum. They provide tiny doses of nicotine that help some smokers to gradually stop the habit.

Questions

1. What does the diaphragm do during breathing in?
2. What is the function of the alveoli?
3. What are the advantages of breathing in through the nose rather than through the mouth?

The circulation

You need to know

- the structure of the heart and how it pumps blood around the body;
- the main features of the circulatory system;
- how red blood cells transport oxygen;
- the structure and function of arteries and veins;
- about the circulation problems associated with our lifestyle;
- how the hormone insulin regulates glucose.

The human heart – a powerful pump

The heart moves blood around the body. It consists of **cardiac muscle**, which never tires, throughout your lifetime.

The heart function sequence is:

- the heart receives deoxygenated blood via the veins;
- it pumps blood to the lungs;
- the blood picks up oxygen at the lungs and carbon dioxide is given up;
- the heart receives oxygenated blood from the lungs;
- it pumps blood all around the body.

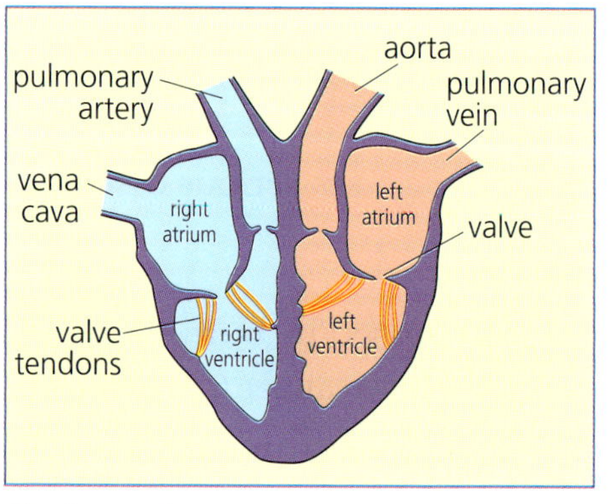

The human heart

The heart valves

- The function of all valves is to make sure that blood moves in **one direction only**. Any attempt by the blood to move backwards and the valve closes tightly.
- The **valve tendons** prevent each atrio-ventricular valve from collapsing back into an atrium.
- **Semi-lunar valves** are in the aorta and pulmonary artery, and prevent back-flow of blood into the atria.

The coronary artery supplies the heart with its own supply of oxygen and glucose.

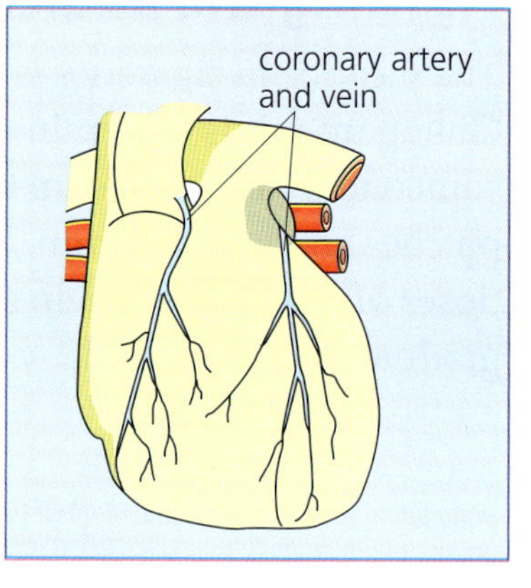

The blood vessels

Arteries have a tough outer wall and a thick layer of smooth muscle. This muscle contracts to help pump blood.

Veins have a tough protective outer wall and a very thin layer of smooth muscle. They have valves to make sure that the blood only travels towards the heart.

Capillaries are very small, thin vessels, just one cell thick, so that substances can pass through easily. Chemicals, e.g. glucose, diffuse out into the tissues, while others, e.g. carbon dioxide, diffuse in from the tissues.

How our lifestyle affects our health

Our diet and behaviour affect our health considerably. We have a choice.

The consumption of **animal fat** (**saturated fat**) can lead to damage to the blood vessels (**arteriosclerosis**):

- yellow fat streaks build up under the lining cells of a vessel;
- an **atheroma** develops that is built up from cholesterol absorbed from blood;
- the atheroma develops into a white fibrous lump;
- eventually, it raises the blood pressure and can cause a blockage.

Heart disease – a possible cause

- A **thrombosis** (blood clot) may block a coronary vessel, preventing supplies such as oxygen reaching the heart.
- If part of the heart is deprived of oxygen, it causes a sharp pain (**angina**).

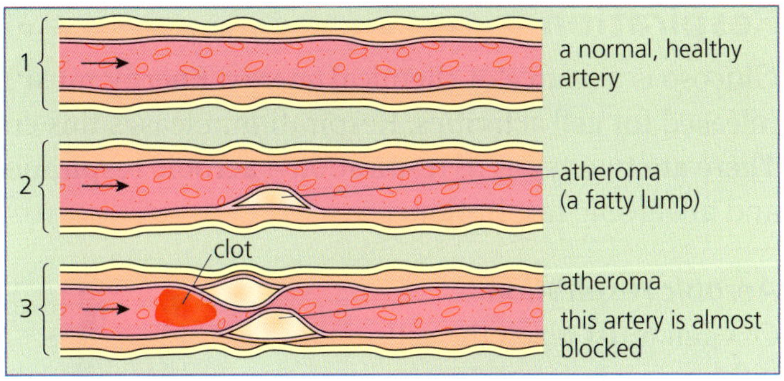

- This pain is a warning to seek medical help.
- If not treated, a total blockage may occur, resulting in a **heart attack**, which can be fatal.

Remember that smoking also damages your blood vessels. They become less elastic and can sometimes leak, causing internal bleeding (haemorrhage).

Blood sugar (glucose) – the full story

We may eat a chocolate bar, full of glucose, or a slice of bread high in starch. Both foods result in the absorption of a high level of glucose into the blood.
Insulin has the following effects:

- it reduces the amount of glucose in the blood
- it allows glucose into cells where it is respired to release energy;
- it allows excess glucose into the liver;
- in the liver glucose is changed into glycogen;
- glycogen is an energy store;
- glycogen can later be changed back to glucose, when the person has a low level of glucose in the blood.

Changing the glycogen back to glucose is controlled by a different hormone.

Questions

1 What is the function of a valve between an atrium and a ventricle in the heart?
2 Name the lower chambers of the heart.
3 What is the function of the muscle in an artery?

Respiration, energy and exercise

You need to know

- ✔ about the processes of aerobic and anaerobic respiration;
- ✔ about the repayment of oxygen debt created by anaerobic respiration;
- ✔ about the misuse of steroid drugs.

Respiration

Glucose is a source of chemical energy. Energy must be released for cell activities. Respiration releases this energy. There are two types of respiration – aerobic respiration and anaerobic respiration.

Aerobic respiration

Oxygen must reach the cells if this process is to take place. Oxygen diffuses from the red blood cells through capillary walls into cells. Aerobic respiration takes place in cytoplasm plus the mitochondria.

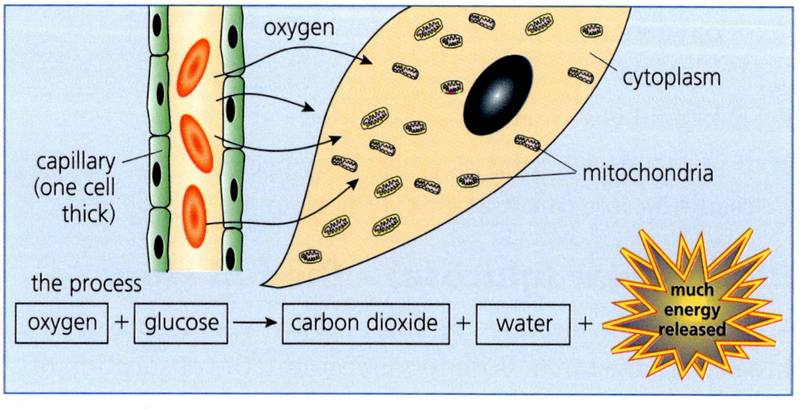

The process of aerobic respiration

How do heart rate and breathing rate affect aerobic respiration?

When exercising or under stress, adrenaline is produced by the adrenal glands. This increases both the heart rate and the breathing rate. As a result, beginning at the lungs:

- more oxygen diffuses into the blood;
- oxygen is transported to the muscles more quickly;
- the rate of respiration increases as more oxygen and more glucose reach the cells.

At the same time, carbon dioxide must be excreted faster:

- more carbon dioxide diffuses into the blood from the cells;
- carbon dioxide is transported to the lungs more quickly;
- more carbon dioxide diffuses into alveoli of the lungs to be lost during breathing out.

Think about this logically – as you breathe in and out more often you are bound to take in more oxygen and give out more carbon dioxide.

Anaerobic respiration

Sometimes your body needs energy faster than the oxygen can get to your cells. This may happen when you run a race. Anaerobic respiration releases this extra energy requirement.

Lactic acid quickly builds up in the muscle tissues and some reaches the blood. Build-up of lactic acid can give a pain, known as cramp.

In a long distance race, aerobic respiration is used.

At the end of the race, repayment of oxygen debt takes place. Rapid breathing rate at the end of the race results in a greater supply of oxygen. Most of the lactic acid is oxidised to carbon dioxide and water, releasing energy.

During repayment of oxygen debt, lactic acid is involved in different processes:

Process	Percentage of lactic acid
oxidised to carbon dioxide and water	64
changed to protein	11
changed to glucose	6
changed to glycogen in muscles, liver	19

The following table provides a comparison of aerobic and anaerobic respiration.

	Aerobic respiration	Anaerobic respiration
substrate used	glucose	glucose
energy released	bigger amount	lower amount
waste product(s)	carbon dioxide + water	lactic acid

You will often be asked about the differences between the two processes in an exam

Misuse of steroid drugs

Some young athletes take steroid drugs. They promote muscle growth and improve strength. However, there are major problems with the use of these hormones – not only are they illegal, but they have long-term side-effects. They can increase the risk of both heart disease and sterility.

Questions

1 Complete the word equation for aerobic respiration
glucose + __________ → carbon dioxide + __________

2 Where does aerobic respiration take place?

3 Which type of respiration releases the most energy?

Inherited diseases

You need to know

- the symptoms of a range of inherited disorders;
- how gene therapy can be used to treat some genetic disorders;
- how genetic counselling can help people make informed decisions.

Harmful microorganisms cause many common diseases, but some diseases are caused by alleles that do not function properly. They are passed on from parents to their children.

Cystic fibrosis is an inherited disease carried by a recessive allele. Its characteristics are:

- a thick sticky mucus is produced in the lungs;
- breathing is difficult;
- the sticky mucus must be coughed up each day to relieve breathing difficulty;
- fluid that lubricates the first part of the small intestine is also thick and sticky;
- food passes through the intestines with greater difficulty and digestion is inhibited.

We inherit a genetic disease when a gene does not function correctly. Every nucleus in our body cells has the gene. **Gene therapy** is the attempt to replace defective genes with copies of the healthy ones. Gene therapy is in the early days of development. In the case of cystic fibrosis, healthy genes are sprayed into the lungs via an aerosol. Surface cells receive the healthy gene and no longer produce the sticky mucus. Unfortunately, this treatment is only effective for about a month. It is still experimental.

Remember a gene is a section of DNA that has a specific function. Each gene has a number of different forms, e.g. "normal mucus" and "cystic mucus".

Replacement of every gene that does not function correctly is an extremely difficult task and not yet achieved.

Sickle cell anaemia is another inherited disease carried by a recessive allele. In people who suffer from the condition, normal haemoglobin (dominant) is replaced by a different type, haemoglobin-S. The characteristics of sickle cell anaemia are:

- red blood cells distort and become sickle-shaped;
- these cells are less efficient than normal red blood cells at transporting oxygen;
- as a result, the patient suffers from anaemia;
- the sickle red cells tend to "log-jam" and block capillaries, depriving cells of oxygen;
- some people have the normal allele and the sickle cell allele – this is known as sickle cell trait, because some of the red blood cells are normal and some are sickle-shaped (30–40%), but the condition is not life-threatening;
- some people inherit sickle alleles from both parents – this is often fatal.

People who have both alleles which are cystic, often die.

Questions

1. Describe how cystic fibrosis sufferers can be helped by gene therapy.
2. How does sickle cell anaemia result in less oxygen transport in the blood?
3. How can sickled red blood cells stop blood flow?

Practice module test

You will have 17 minutes to answer these questions

1 Which of these substances is produced in an athlete's muscles during anaerobic respiration?

- **A** lactic acid
- **B** glucose
- **C** carbon dioxide
- **D** oxygen

2 The diagram shows a section through the chest. Part X is:

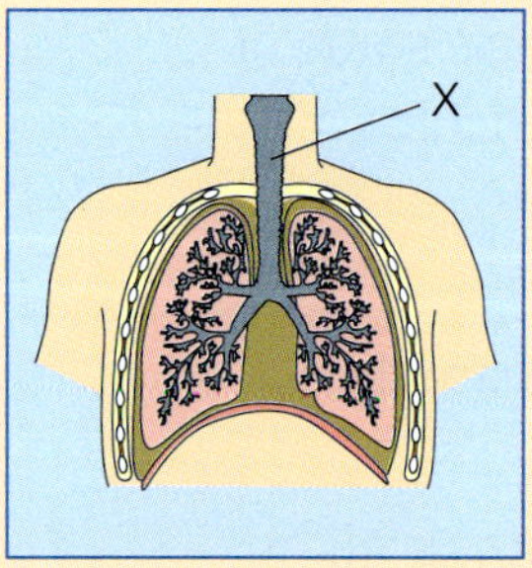

- **A** bronchus
- **B** bronchiole
- **C** windpipe (trachea)
- **D** diaphragm

3 During **breathing in** the condition of the rib cage and diaphragm are shown by which row below (**A**, **B**, **C** or **D**)?

	Rib cage	Diaphragm
A	upwards and outwards	moves up
B	upwards and outwards	moves down
C	downwards and inwards	moves up
D	downwards and inwards	moves down

4 Which of the following drugs is taken illegally by some athletes to improve their performance?

- **A** insulin
- **B** paracetamol
- **C** aspirin
- **D** steroids

5 During exercise, the heart rate:

- **A** rises
- **B** falls
- **C** remains at the same level
- **D** decreases then increases

6 Blood vessels can become blocked by:

- **A** eating fatty foods
- **B** exercising too much
- **C** eating too much fibre
- **D** avoiding fried foods

7 The smallest blood vessel is:

- **A** an artery
- **B** a vein
- **C** an arteriole
- **D** a capillary

8 The disease sickle cell anaemia reduces the efficiency of transporting:

- **A** oxygen
- **B** carbon dioxide
- **C** nitrogen
- **D** glucose

9 Which TWO useful substances are transported to the heart by the coronary artery?

- **A** urea and oxygen
- **B** oxygen and carbon dioxide
- **C** glucose and carbon dioxide
- **D** glucose and oxygen

10 In an organism energy is released by:

- **A** digestion
- **B** respiration
- **C** breathing in
- **D** breathing out

11 Oxygen passes from the air in the lungs into the blood by:

- **A** osmosis
- **B** diffusion
- **C** respiration
- **D** breathing in

12 Look at the diagram at the top of the next page. Which vessel takes deoxygenated blood into the heart?

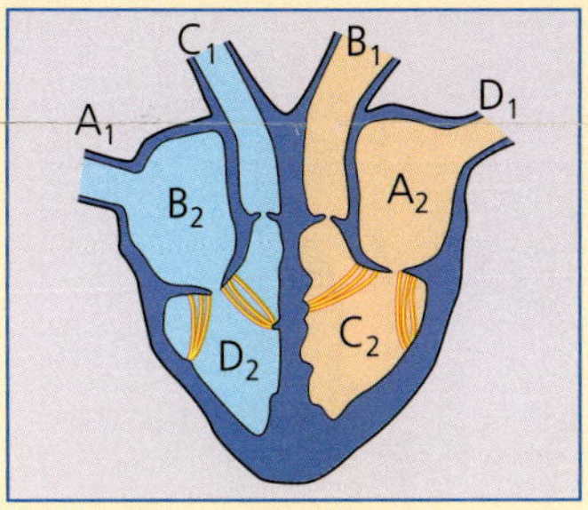

A vena cava (A_1)
B aorta (B_1)
C pulmonary artery (C_1)
D pulmonary vein (D_1)

13 Look at the diagram of the heart above. Which chamber contracts to pump oxygenated blood to most parts of the body?

A left atrium (A_2)
B right atrium (B_2)
C left ventricle (C_2)
D right ventricle (D_2)

14 The diagram below shows some of the cells found in the lining of the lungs. The cilia move backwards and forwards to:

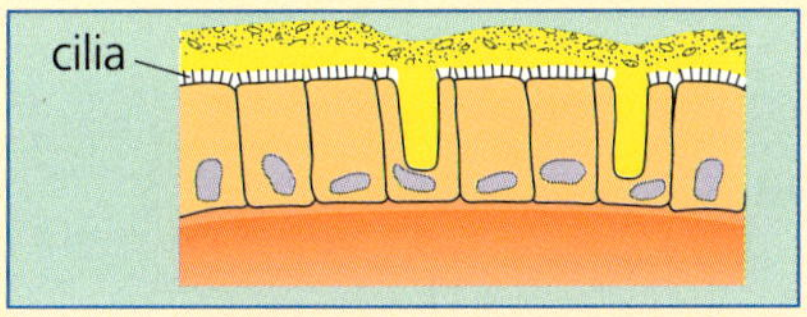

A kill bacteria
B cool down the air in the lungs
C move the mucus to the throat area
D circulate the air in the lungs

15 Cells lining the lungs of smokers become covered in tar. Tar is harmful. Which of the following is **not** true?

A it slows down diffusion of oxygen into the blood
B it slows down diffusion of carbon dioxide out of the blood
C it causes cancer
D it is addictive

16 After each meal, which hormone results in a decrease in glucose in the blood?

A insulin
B glucagon
C adrenaline
D testosterone

17 The diagram below shows a section through a red blood cell. Red blood cells can transport a lot of oxygen because they:

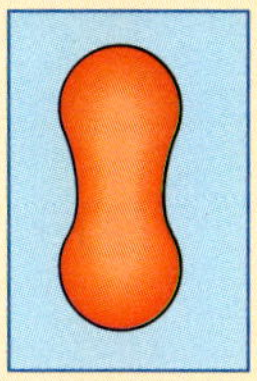

A have a low surface area to volume ratio
B contain haemoglobin
C have a large nucleus
D have a cell membrane

18 The diagram below shows how a lung cell becomes abnormal and increases in number. Which disease is shown by the diagram?

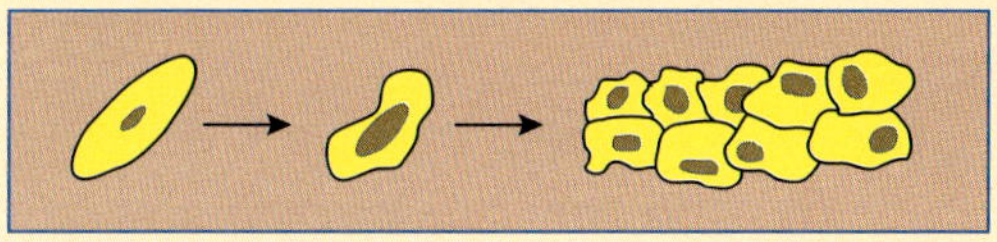

A emphysema
B bronchitis
C cancer
D pneumoconiosis

19 The diagram shows a red blood cell from a person suffering from a genetic disease. What is the disease?

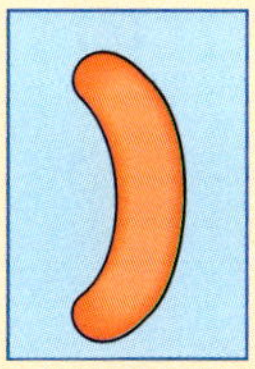

A cystic fibrosis
B sickle cell anaemia
C influenza
D bronchitis

20 In a long distance race we respire aerobically. This produces a lot of:

A oxygen
B carbon dioxide
C glucose
D lactic acid

Answers to these questions can be found on pages 140–144

Getting it right

1 The diagram below shows the human heart. Use information in the diagram and your own knowledge to answer the following questions.

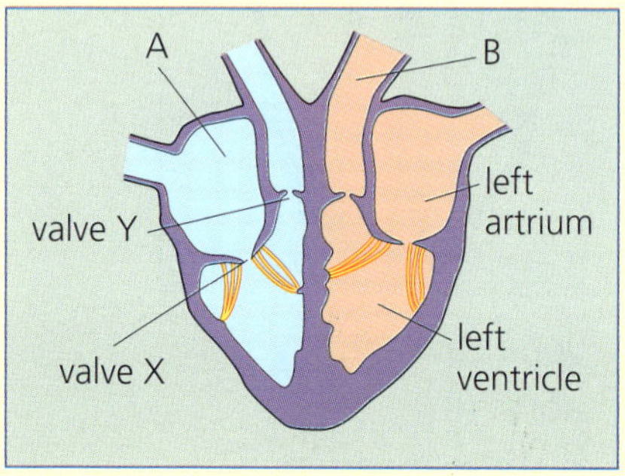

(a) Name parts A and B.

A = right atrium, B = aorta **[2]**

(b) Why does the left atrium have much thinner muscular walls than the left ventricle?

The atrium pumps blood to the ventricle below, a short distance. The left ventricle pumps blood a greater distance, around the body. **[2]**

(c) Which side of the heart contains deoxygenated blood?

The right. **[1]**

(d) What happens to valve X when

(i) the right atrium contracts, and the right ventricle relaxes?

Valve X opens. **[1]**

(ii) the right atrium relaxes, and the right ventricle contracts?

Valve X closes. **[1]**

(e) What is the function of:

(i) valves X and Y?

Make sure that blood goes from the atrim to the ventricle – prevents back-flow of blood. **[1]**

(ii) heart tendons?

They stop the valves from being pushed back into the atria. **[1]**

(f) Some people eat a lot of animal fat in their diet. How can this affect the heart?

Cholesterol builds up in the arteries; can result in a blockage; causes hear attack. **[3]**

Chemicals and the Earth

The first topic in this module is about how metals are extracted from their ores. We then look at the metals in the middle of the periodic table – the transition metals. The third topic is on alkali metals, a family of reactive metals in Group 1. We then go on to look at rocks – important building materials and a source of many other materials. In the final topic we look at the atmosphere and the gases in the atmosphere.

Extracting metals from their ores

You need to know

- about the uses of iron/steel, aluminium and copper;
- how metals are extracted from their ores, relating the method to the position of the metal in the order of reactivity;
- how iron and aluminium are extracted and how copper is purified by electrolysis.

Uses of metals

The table on the right gives some common uses of iron/steel, aluminium and copper.

Metal	Common uses
iron/steel	ships, cars, bridges
aluminium	aeroplanes, cooking foil, overhead power cables
copper	electrical wiring, water pipes

Extraction of metals

Most metals are found in the Earth in metal compounds. These are mixed with other minerals in **ores**.

Metals are usually extracted from their ores by **reduction** reactions. Reduction is a reaction in which oxygen is lost. For example, copper oxide is reduced to copper when oxygen is removed.

Reactivity series of metals

potassium
sodium
calcium
magnesium
aluminium
zinc
iron
lead
copper
gold

Position of metal in reactivity series	Example	Method of extraction
high	aluminium	electrolysis
middle	iron	reduction with carbon or carbon monoxide
low	gold	metal uncombined in the Earth

Metals high in the reactivity series form stable compounds. These are difficult to split up and require a reduction process that provides a large amount of energy, e.g. electrolysis.

Extraction of aluminium

Aluminium is extracted from purified **bauxite** (aluminium oxide) by electrolysis. The diagram shows a cell used to extract aluminium.

The electrolyte is aluminium oxide dissolved in molten cryolite. The lining of the cell is made of carbon and this acts as the cathode (negative electrode). The anodes (positive electrodes) are made of carbon.

aluminium oxide → aluminium (at cathode) + oxygen (at anode)

The anodes burn away and have to be replaced.

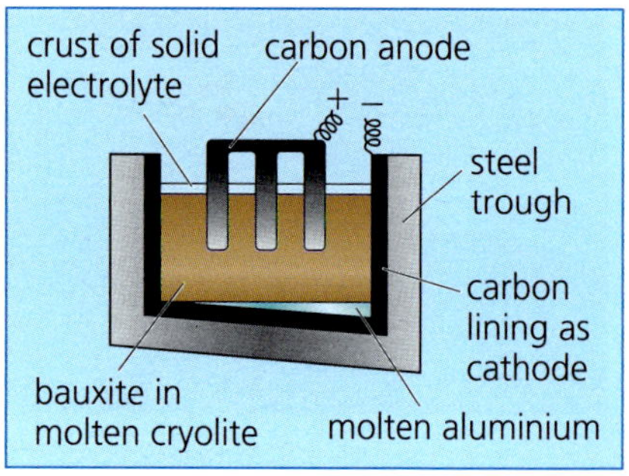

An aluminium extraction cell

Extraction of iron

Iron is extracted from iron ore by reduction in a blast furnace. The furnace is loaded with iron ore, coke and limestone and then heated with blasts of hot air.

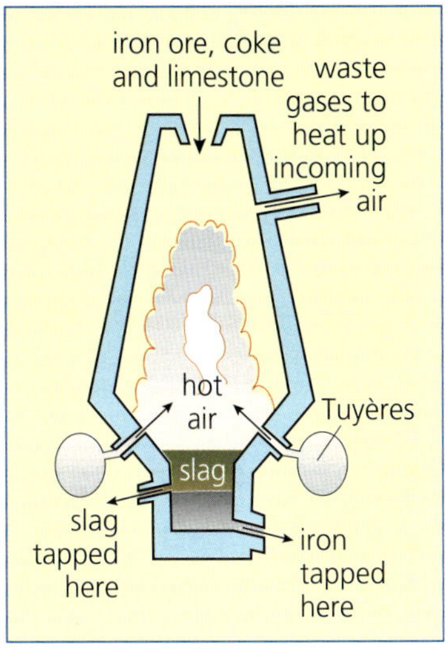

A blast furnace

The products of the furnace are molten iron and slag. They are tapped off at the bottom of the furnace. Most of the iron is turned into steel. The slag is used as a phosphorus fertiliser and for road chippings.

The main reactions taking place in the furnace can be summarised as:

1. **carbon + oxygen → carbon dioxide**
2. **carbon dioxide + carbon → carbon monoxide**
3. **iron oxide + carbon monoxide → iron + carbon dioxide**
4. **calcium carbonate → calcium oxide + carbon dioxide**
5. **calcium oxide + silicon dioxide → calcium silicate**

Purification of copper by electrolysis

Copper is purified by electrolysis. The impure copper is used to make the anode (positive electrode) in the cell. The cathode (negative electrode) is pure copper. The electrolyte is copper(II) sulphate solution.

During the electrolysis, the anode dissolves and pure copper is deposited on the cathode. The impurities sink to the bottom of the cell and collect as anode mud.

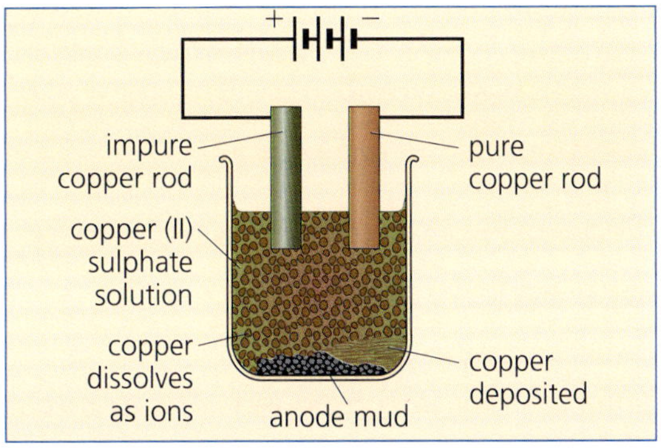

Purification of copper

Questions

1 Which metal in the list could be extracted by electrolysis?

gold lead sodium zinc

2 What three materials are put into the blast furnace in the production of iron?

3 What name is given to a reaction that removes oxygen from a compound?

4 Copper(II) sulphate solution contains copper ions. What happens to these copper ions during electrolysis?

Transition metals

You need to know

- where transition metals are found in the periodic table;
- the physical properties of iron and copper;
- that transition metal compounds are coloured;
- that transition metals and transition metal compounds are catalysts.

Where are transition metals in the periodic table?

Transition metals are found in a block between Groups 2 and 3 in the periodic table.

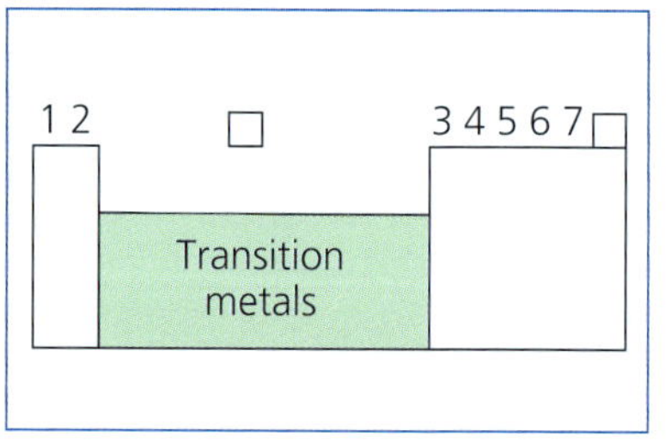

Position of transition metals in the periodic table

Physical properties of iron and copper

Iron and copper are examples of transition metals. They have the typical properties of transition metals:

- high melting points;
- good conductors of heat and electricity;
- high density.

You will find other examples in this book of the use of transition metals and their compounds as catalysts.

Transition metals form coloured compounds

Many transition metal compounds are coloured. For example, copper(II) compounds are blue e.g. copper(II) sulphate. Iron(II) compounds are pale green and iron(III) compounds are red-brown.

Transition metals and their compounds are catalysts

Most common catalysts are either transition metals or transition metal compounds. For example, the catalyst for the decomposition of hydrogen peroxide is manganese(IV) oxide.

Questions

The table gives some facts about three metals that have been given the letters A, B and C.

Metal	Melting point (°C)	Density (g/cm^3)	Colour of sulphate
A	64	0.86	colourless
B	420	7.1	colourless
C	1890	7.2	green

1 Which of the three metals is definitely a transition metal?

2 Which one is definitely **not** a transition metal?

Alkali metals

You need to know

- that they are found in Group 1 of the periodic table;
- that alkali metals have comparatively low melting points and are soft;
- about the reactions of alkali metals with water;
- how to describe and predict the reactivity of the alkali metals.

Lithium, sodium and potassium are alkali metals. They are found in Group 1 of the periodic table. They have low melting points and are soft. They are stored under paraffin because they are so reactive.

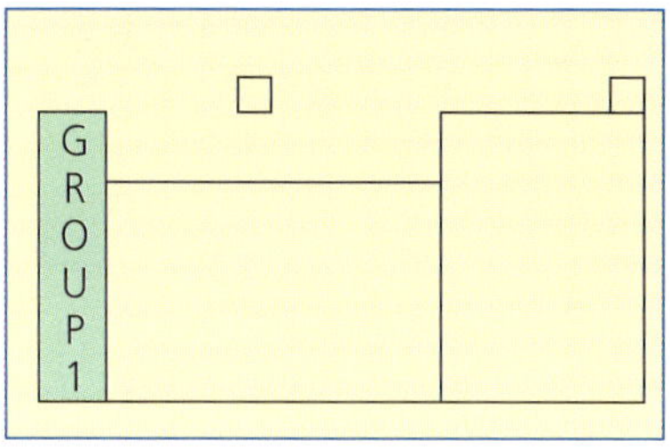

Outline periodic table showing Group 1

Alkali metal	Symbol	Melting point (°C)	Hard or soft
lithium	Li	180	fairly soft
sodium	Na	98	soft
potassium	K	64	very soft

The reactions of alkali metals with water

Alkali metals react with cold water. If a piece of sodium is dropped onto water:

- it floats;
- it melts and a molten ball of sodium is formed;
- it fizzes and shoots about the surface;
- it produces a colourless gas;
- the remaining solution is alkaline ($pH > 7$);

The reaction produces an alkali (sodium hydroxide) and hydrogen gas.

The reactivity of alkali metals increases down the group. With potassium, for example, the hydrogen catches alight and burns with a pinkish-lilac flame.

Questions

1 When sodium is added to water, what causes Universal Indicator to turn purple?

2 Complete the word equations below.

lithium + water → __________ + __________

potassium + water → __________ + __________

3 Rubidium is an alkali metal below potassium in the periodic table. Would you expect it to be more or less reactive than potassium?

Rocks and their uses

You need to know

- ✔ the products of the electrolysis of sodium chloride solution and the uses of these products;
- ✔ that igneous rocks are produced as the magma cools and crystallises;
- ✔ that the rate of cooling determines the size of crystals in an igneous rock;
- ✔ that sedimentary rocks are formed from other rocks and the lower down a layer of sedimentary rock is the older it is;
- ✔ that fossils can be used to date rocks;
- ✔ that metamorphic rocks are formed by the action of heat and pressure on existing rocks.

Electrolysis of concentrated sodium chloride solution

Electrolysis of concentrated sodium chloride solution produces **sodium hydroxide**, **chlorine** and **hydrogen**.

We use sodium hydroxide for making bleach, soap, paper and textile fibres and for drain cleaning. We use chlorine for purification of water supplies, for bleaching and killing bacteria in swimming baths. Hydrogen is used for making margarine and ammonia.

Igneous rocks

Igneous rocks, e.g. granite and basalt, are formed when the magma crystallises. Igneous rocks do not contain fossils – this is evidence that these rocks have been formed directly from the magma.

Basalt is formed when the magma crystallises quickly and produces small interlocking crystals.

Granite is formed when the magma crystallises slowly inside the Earth. Granite consists of larger crystals.

Sedimentary rocks

When weathering and erosion break down existing rocks, sediments are produced. These are transported by rivers into the sea, where they are deposited. These sediments are then compressed and cemented together to form new sedimentary rocks. Sedimentary rocks include limestone and sandstone.

Sedimentary rocks can contain fossils and the nature of the fossils present can be used to date rocks.

In a succession of rocks, for example a cliff face, the older the rock is the lower down it is in the Earth.

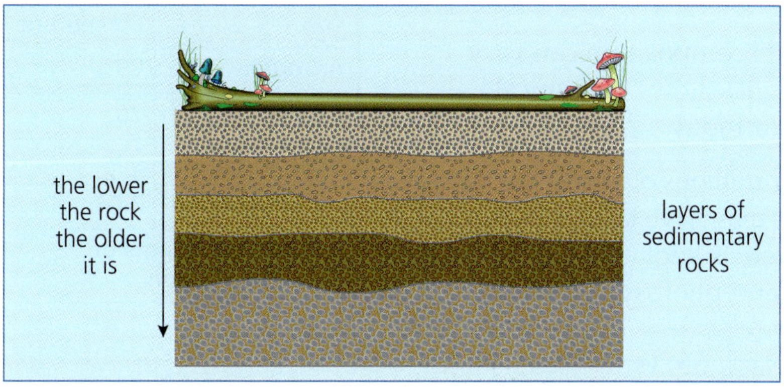

Succession of layers of rock

Metamorphic rocks

The effect of high temperature and high pressure on existing rocks can cause them to change and form new rocks. Marble, for example, is a metamorphic rock produced by the action of high temperatures and high pressures on limestone. The fact that marble and limestone are both forms of calcium carbonate is evidence that marble is made from limestone.

Questions

Of the three types of rock – granite, limestone and marble:

1. Which rock is a sedimentary rock?
2. Which rock is a metamorphic rock?
3. Which rock is an igneous rock?

Of the three types of rock – igneous, metamorphic and sedimentary:

4. Which type of rock cannot be crystalline or contain fossils?

The atmosphere and the gases in it

You need to know

- how and why the composition of the atmosphere has changed;
- how the composition of the atmosphere is kept in balance;
- that nitrogen and hydrogen combine to form ammonia;
- that nitrogen fertilisers can promote growth in plants;
- that neutralising ammonia produces a fertiliser;
- that over-use of nitrogen fertilisers can cause environmental problems;
- that noble gases are inert because their atoms have full electron shells;
- about some of the uses of noble gases.

The atmosphere

Air is a mixture of gases and so its composition can vary from place to place. The table (right) shows the typical composition of a sample of dry air today.

Gas	Percentage
nitrogen	79
oxygen	20
argon	0.9
carbon dioxide	0.04
plus small amounts of helium and neon	

The atmosphere has changed over millions of years. The table (below) shows how these changes may have taken place. The composition of the atmosphere is kept constant because respiration, combustion rusting and photosynthesis produces it again.

Change	Effect on the atmosphere
the first atmosphere	consisted mainly of **hydrogen** and **helium**
volcanoes started to erupt	mostly **carbon dioxide** and **water vapour** entering the atmosphere; smaller quantities of **methane** and **ammonia**
Earth cools	water vapour condenses to **liquid water**. Oceans start to form
nitrifying and denitrifying bacteria start to work	ammonia converted to **nitrates** and nitrates are converted into **nitrogen** gas
methane in the atmosphere burns	**carbon dioxide** is formed
photosynthesis occurs	plants convert carbon dioxide into **oxygen**
burning of fossil fuels	increasing levels of carbon dioxide

Using nitrogen in the air to make ammonia

Nitrogen and hydrogen react from ammonia in the Haber process.

We obtain nitrogen from fractional distillation of liquid air and hydrogen by the cracking of hydrocarbons.

The mixture of hydrogen and ammonia is passed over an iron catalyst. The conditions are high pressures and a temperature of about 45 °C. The reaction is **reversible**.

As a result an **equilibrium** is set up: **nitrogen + hydrogen ⇌ ammonia**

Fertilisers

Nitrogen compounds can act as **fertilisers** to make plants grow better.

Most plants cannot take in nitrogen from the atmosphere but rely on the nitrogen being "fixed" in compounds that they take up through their roots.

Two important nitrogen fertilisers are ammonium nitrate and ammonium sulphate. These can be made by neutralising ammonia with nitric or sulphuric acid:

Fertilisers often have NPK values. This gives the amounts of the three important elements – nitrogen, phosphorus and potassium.

ammonia solution + nitric acid → ammonium nitrate

ammonia solution + sulphuric acid → ammonium sulphate

Overuse of fertilisers can cause environmental problems.

- Excess nitrogen compounds are washed into rivers.
- Bacteria in the water convert ammonia into nitrates.
- Nitrates make the water plants grow better.
- These plants prevent sunlight entering, reducing photosynthesis.
- When the plants die, oxygen is used up.
- Eventually, the water contains no dissolved oxygen and so all fish and river life die.

Noble gases

The noble gases are in Group 8 of the periodic table. They are very unreactive compared to other elements. These inert properties are a result of the fact that all noble gas atoms have a full outer electron shell. The atoms have no tendency to gain or lose electrons.

The table gives some uses of the three common noble gases.

He
Ne
Ar
Kr
Xe
Rn

Noble gas	Uses
helium	air ships, weather balloons
neon	fluorescent light tubes
argon	electric light bulbs

Questions

1 Which gas is present in the largest amounts in air?

2 Which gas is the most reactive gas in the atmosphere?

3 Why does burning of the rainforests threaten to change the composition of the atmosphere?

4 Which two gases react in the Haber process to produce ammonia?

5 One noble gas is much less dense than air. Which one?

Practice module test

You will have 17 minutes to answer these questions

1 Iron is a transition metal. Which of the following statements is true?

A it does not conduct heat
B it does not conduct electricity
C it has a high density
D it has a low melting point

2 Copper is used to make:

A clothes
B shopping bags
C training shoes
D water pipes

3 Helium is used:

A in airships
B in bleaches
C in thermometers
D as a fuel

4 Ammonia is used to make:

A fertilisers
B petrol
C soap
D washing powders

5 Which rock is an igneous rock?

A granite
B limestone
C marble
D sandstone

6 Rock salt is:

A an element
B a metal
C a mixture of compounds
D a pure compound

7 Burning fuel uses up:

A argon
B carbon dioxide
C nitrogen
D oxygen

8 Copper is:

A an alkali metal
B a halogen
C a noble gas
D a transition metal

Questions 9 and 10. Use the list of metals to help you.

sodium – most reactive
calcium
magnesium
aluminium
zinc
iron
lead – least reactive

9 Which metal is extracted from its ore by electrolysis?

A iron
B lead
C sodium
D zinc

10 Which metal is extracted from its ore by reduction with carbon?

A aluminium
B iron
C magnesium
D sodium

11 Ammonia is made in the Haber process from:

A nitrogen and hydrogen
B nitrogen and oxygen
C hydrogen and oxygen
D nitrogen, hydrogen and oxygen

12 The percentage of nitrogen in the atmosphere is approximately:

- **A** 1%
- **B** 4%
- **C** 20%
- **D** 80%

13 Ammonium sulphate is a fertiliser. It is made by reacting ammonia with:

- **A** sulphur
- **B** copper sulphate
- **C** iron sulphide
- **D** sulphuric acid

14 Lithium reacts with cold water to form:

- **A** an acid and hydrogen
- **B** an acid and oxygen
- **C** an alkali and hydrogen
- **D** an alkali and oxygen

15 Sedimentary rocks are produced when fragments of other rocks are:

- **A** compressed and cemented together
- **B** cooled
- **C** heated and compressed
- **D** melted and crystallised

16 Which process produces oxygen?

- **A** combustion
- **B** photosynthesis
- **C** respiration
- **D** rusting

17 Of the three types of rock – igneous rocks, metamorphic rocks and sedimentary rocks – in which would you find fossils?

- **A** sedimentary and metamorphic rocks
- **B** sedimentary and igneous rocks
- **C** igneous and metamorphic rocks
- **D** sedimentary, igneous and metamorphic rocks

18 Sodium hydroxide is used to make:

- **A** baking powder
- **B** soap
- **C** table salt
- **D** toothpaste

19 Electrolysis of concentrated sodium chloride solution produces:

- **A** sodium and chlorine
- **B** sodium hydroxide, hydrogen and chlorine
- **C** sodium hydroxide, oxygen and hydrogen
- **D** sodium hydroxide, chlorine and oxygen

20 A reaction that happens in a blast furnace is:

iron oxide + carbon monoxide
→ iron + carbon dioxide

Which substance is reduced?

- **A** carbon dioxide
- **B** carbon monoxide
- **C** iron
- **D** iron oxide

Answers to these questions can be found on pages 140–144

Getting it right

1 **(a)** Draw a straight line from each metal in List A to its use in List B

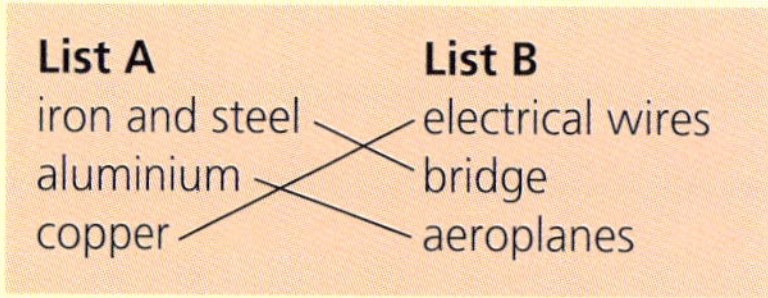

[2]

Two marks are awarded for three correct lines as shown; one mark for one or two lines correct.

(b) The table gives some information about three metals, X, Y and Z.

Metal	Melting point (°C)	Conductor of heat and electricity	Density (g/cm^3)	Colour of sulphate
X	98	good	0.97	white
Y	1890	good	7.19	green
Z	650	good	1.74	white

Which one is a transition metal? Explain the reasons for your choice.

Y is the transition metal. It has a high melting point. It has a high density. It has a coloured compound (the sulphate). **[5]**

One mark is awarded for presenting relevant information in a form that suits its purpose. Notice that the conductivity of X, Y and Z can give no distinction.

2 **(a)** The composition of the atmosphere is kept approximately in balance by several different processes. Explain how these processes do this.

Combustion and respiration use up oxygen and produce carbon dioxide. Photosynthesis absorbs carbon dioxide and produces oxygen. Seas and oceans absorb carbon dioxide. **[4]**

Three marks in (a) are testing Ideas and Evidence. They are dealing with environmental issues. One mark is allocated for QWC. It is awarded if candidates use correct spelling, punctuation and grammar to make the meaning clear.

(b) Suggest two environmental changes that might alter the balance.

Cutting down forests will reduce photosynthesis. 2. Pollution of the seas might reduce the absorption of carbon dioxide. **[2]**

There may be other acceptable answers. The word 'suggest' means there may be a variety of possible answers.

Understanding chemical reactions

The first topic in this module is intended to extend your understanding of the structure of the atom and the particles that make up atoms. The second topic looks at the types of forces holding atoms together. The third topic is about energy transfers that take place when reactions occur. In the final topic, relative atomic masses are used to calculate the relative formula masses of simple compounds.

Atoms and isotopes

You need to know

- the relative charges and masses of protons, neutrons and electrons;
- the meanings of atomic mass and atomic number;
- how to work out the number of protons, neutrons and electrons in an atom;
- that some elements can exist in different isotopes that have the same number of protons but different numbers of neutrons
- how to work out the relative formula mass of an element.

Protons, neutrons and electrons

All atoms are made up of three types of particle – protons, neutrons and electrons. The table below gives information about these three particles.

Atoms are the smallest part of an element that can exist alone.

Particle	Mass	Charge
proton, p	1 unit	+1
neutron, n	1 unit	0
electron, e	negligible	−1

All the atoms in an element contain the same number of protons. All atoms are neutral.

Atoms must contain equal numbers of protons and electrons.

The protons and neutrons in an atom are tightly packed together in the **nucleus**. The nucleus of an atom is positively charged.

Electrons are arranged in shells around the nucleus.

Each atom has a **mass number** and an **atomic number**. The mass number is the number of protons and neutrons in the nucleus of the atom. The atomic number is the number of protons in the nucleus of the atom.

For example, a sodium atom has a mass number of 23 and an atomic number of 11. This means that the nucleus of a sodium atom contains 11 protons and (23–11), i.e. 12 neutrons. There are 11 electrons around the nucleus.

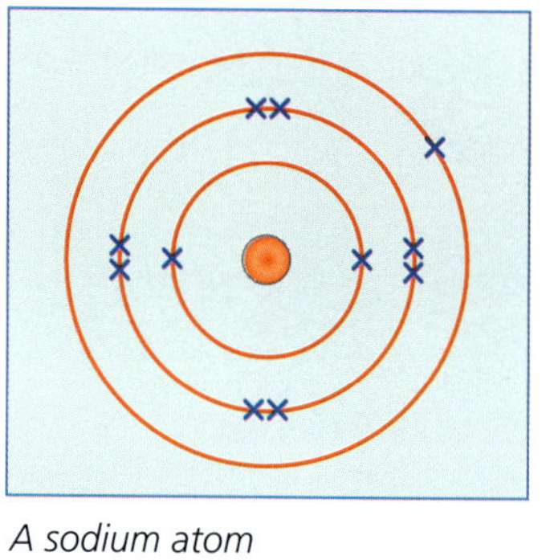

A sodium atom

Isotopes

Hydrogen gas is made up of hydrogen atoms only. But there are three different types of hydrogen atom – they are all hydrogen atoms because they contain one proton and one electron, but they contain different numbers of neutrons.

Atoms of the same element containing different numbers of neutrons are called **isotopes**.

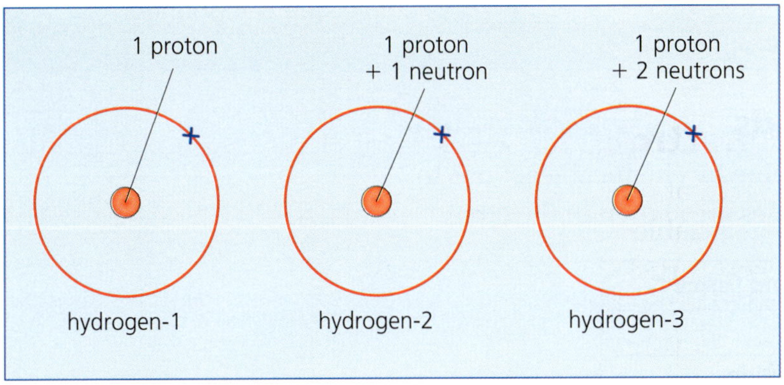

The three isotopes of hydrogen

Students often confuse isotope with isomer and allotrope – make sure you know the difference.

Questions

A phosphorus atom has an atomic number of 15 and a mass number of 31.

1 How many protons does a phosphorus atom contain?

2 How many electrons does a phosphorus atom contain?

3 How many neutrons does a phosphorus atom contain?

Oxygen has two isotopes – oxygen-16 and oxygen-18.

4 Each oxygen isotope has atoms containing the same number of protons and electrons. How many?

5 What is the number of neutrons in each isotope?

Chemical bonds

You need to know

- ✔ that chemical bonding involves transfer or sharing of electrons;
- ✔ that ionic bonds are formed between metal and non-metal atoms, e.g. sodium and chlorine forming sodium chloride;
- ✔ that compounds containing ionic bonding have lattice structures;
- ✔ about the physical properties of ionic compounds;
- ✔ that covalent bonds are formed between atoms of non-metals to produce simple molecules;
- ✔ about the physical properties of simple molecular compounds.

Elements to compounds

A mixture of elements can combine by chemical reactions to form **compounds**. Some examples are shown in the table.

Elements mixed	Compound formed
hydrogen and oxygen	water
iron and sulphur	iron sulphide
carbon and oxygen	carbon dioxide
sodium and chlorine	sodium chloride

A compound has different properties from the elements that make it up.

Atoms of different elements can be joined together by two different types of bonding – ionic and covalent bonding.

Ionic bonding

Ionic bonding joins metal and non-metal atoms together. It involves a complete transfer of one or more electrons.
Sodium chloride is an example.

A complete transfer of one electron from a sodium atom to a chlorine atom forms two **ions**. The sodium ion has a positive charge and the chloride ion has a negative charge. Strong electrostatic forces hold the two ions together.

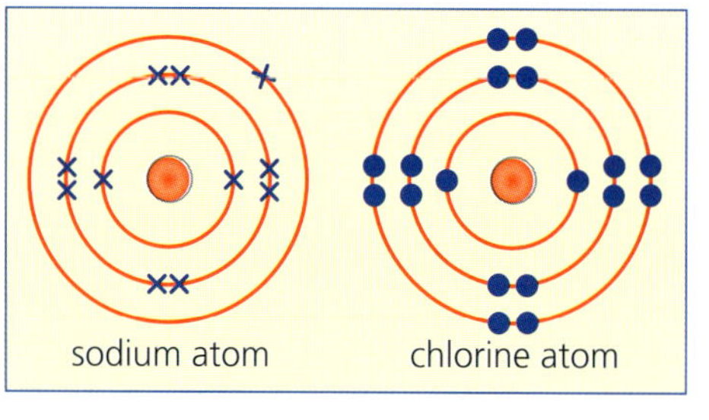

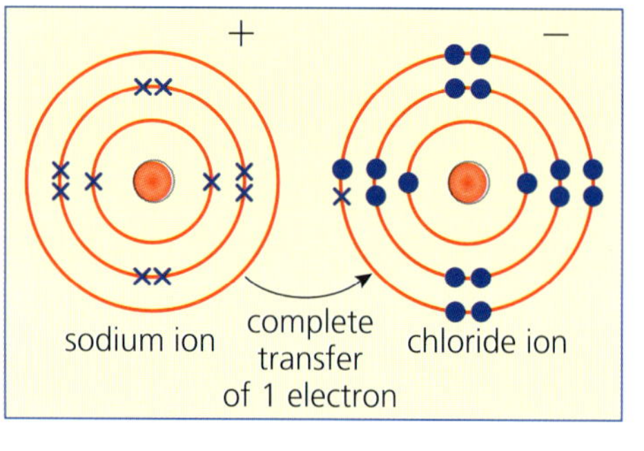

An ion is an atom or group of atoms with a positive or negative charge.

It is wrong to speak of a sodium chloride molecule. This would assume that one sodium ion joins with one chloride ion.

Property	Result for ionic compound
state	solid
melting point	high because of strong forces between ions
solubility in water	usually good
solubility in hydrocarbon solvent	poor

A large number of sodium ions and the same number of chloride ions are joined together in an ionic **lattice**.

The table gives some properties of compounds containing ionic bonding.

Another example of ionic bonding is magnesium oxide.

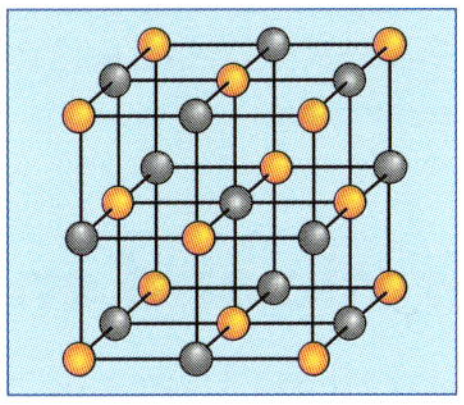

Sodium chloride lattice

Covalent bonding

Covalent bonding usually involves joining non-metal atoms together by **sharing** electrons.

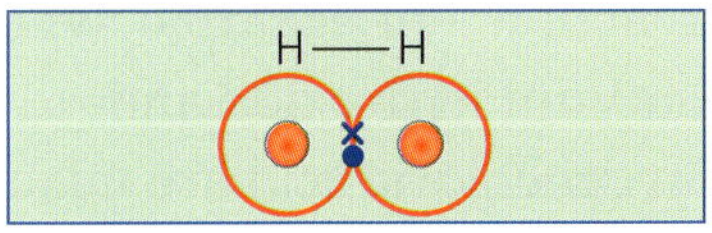

Covalent bonding in hydrogen

The simplest example is a hydrogen molecule, formed when two atoms of hydrogen join together. Each hydrogen atom gives one electron and the pair of electrons is shared to form a **covalent bond**.

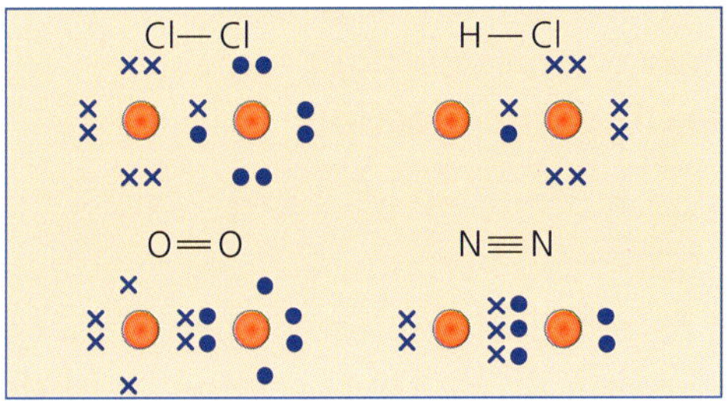

Chlorine, hydrogen chloride, oxygen and nitrogen molecules

Other examples of covalent bonding are chlorine, hydrogen chloride, oxygen and nitrogen.

The table gives some properties of compounds containing covalent bonding.

Property	Result for covalent compound containing molecules
state	usually gas
boiling point	very low
solubility in water	poor (exception HCl)
solubility in hydrocarbon solvent	good

Questions

1 Which type of bonding would be expected in (a) potassium oxide and (b) hydrogen oxide?
2 Which type of bonding involves a complete transfer of electrons?
3 Which type of bonding leads to the formation of molecules?
4 Metal ions are positively charged. True or false?

Energy transfers

You need to know

- that temperature changes may be seen during reactions;
- that an exothermic reaction is a reaction where energy is given out and an endothermic reaction is a reaction where energy is taken in from the surroundings.
- how to work out the relative formula mass of a simple compound using relative atomic masses.

Exothermic and endothermic reactions

In some reactions there is a rise in temperature during the reaction. For example, when sodium hydroxide and hydrochloric acid are mixed, the temperature rises. This shows that the reaction is giving out energy. It is called an **exothermic reaction**.

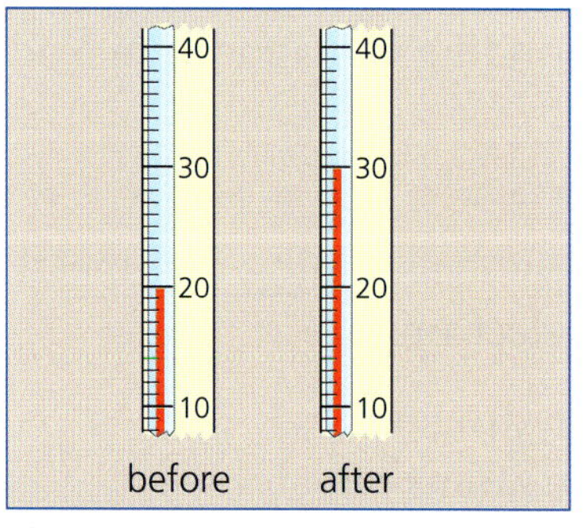

Thermometers showing temperature rise

When dilute hydrochloric acid is added to a carbonate, there is a slight fall in temperature. The reaction is taking in some energy from the surroundings. This is called an **endothermic reaction**.

There are few examples of endothermic reactions. At one time scientists thought that endothermic reactions were impossible because they could not find any.

Using chemical equations

Relative atomic mass

The **relative atomic mass** of an element is the number of times an atom of an element is heavier than the mass of a hydrogen atom.

Magnesium has a relative atomic mass of 24. This means a magnesium atom is 24 times heavier than a hydrogen atom.

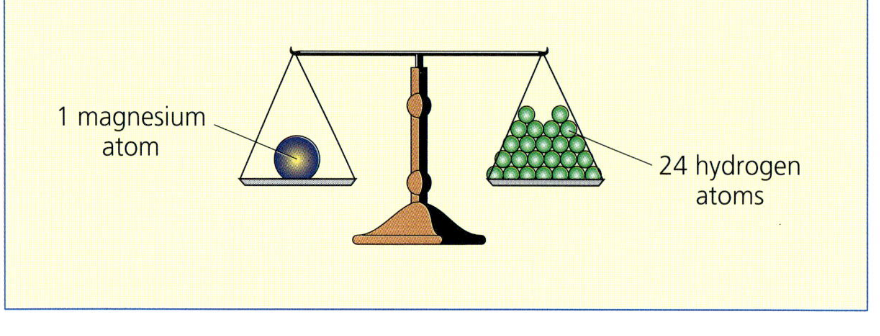

Relative formula mass

The **relative formula mass** of a simple compound is the number of times one molecule of the compound is heavier than the mass of a hydrogen atom.

You can work this out by adding the appropriate relative atomic masses. For example, to find the relative formula mass of water, H_2O:

(Relative atomic masses: O = 16, H = 1)

There are two atoms of hydrogen and one atom of oxygen. So, the relative formula mass of water = $(2 \times 1) + 16 = 18$

You do not have to remember relative atomic masses. They will be given to you when you need them. For example:
(Relative atomic mass: S = 32, O = 16)

Questions

1 The reaction for respiration in a cell is

glucose + oxygen → carbon dioxide + water

This reaction is exothermic. Finish the equation by adding '+ energy' on the correct side.

2 The equation for photosynthesis is

carbon dioxide + water → glucose + oxygen

Is this reaction exothermic or endothermic?

3 Is the combustion of carbon exothermic or endothermic?

The relative atomic masses of carbon and magnesium are 12 and 24.

4 How many times heavier is a carbon atom than a hydrogen atom?

5 How many times heavier is a magnesium atom than a carbon atom?

6 What is the relative formula mass of carbon dioxide, CO_2?
(Relative atomic masses: C = 12, O = 16)

7 What is the relative formula mass of ammonia, NH_3?
(Relative atomic masses: N = 14, H = 1)

Practice module test

You will have 17 minutes to answer these questions

1 When iron and sulphur react, atoms of the two elements:

A expand
B join
C melt
D separate

2 Which of the following is positively charged?

A atom
B electron
C neutron
D nucleus

3 An exothermic reaction takes place when two solutions are mixed. Which of the following statements is true?

A the temperature of the mixture of solutions falls
B the temperature of the mixture of solutions rises
C a gas is produced
D the mixture of solutions changes colour

4 Sodium has an atomic number of 11 and a mass number of 23. A sodium atom contains:

A 11 protons
B 12 protons
C 12 electrons
D 23 neutrons

5 Ionic bonding involves:

A electrons being shared between two metal atoms
B electrons being shared between two non-metal atoms
C electrons being transferred from a non-metal atom to a metal atom
D electrons being transferred from a metal atom to a non-metal atom

Questions 6–8

Use the diagram to help you.

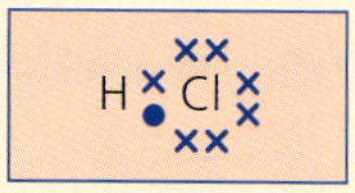

6 The diagram shows a hydrogen chloride:

A atom
B ion
C molecule
D nucleus

7 The dots and crosses represent:

A atoms
B bonds
C electrons
D protons

8 Dry hydrogen chloride at room temperature and atmospheric pressure is a:

A gas
B liquid
C solid
D solution

9 The number of protons in the nucleus of an atom is given by the:

A atomic mass
B atomic number
C mass number
D relative atomic mass

10 Which of the following contains ionic bonding?

A hydrogen
B carbon
C magnesium oxide
D water

11 Which of the following is an ion?

- **A** C
- **B** CO_2
- **C** CO_3^{2-}
- **D** CH_4

Questions 12 and 13. Use the table below to answer these questions.

	Atomic number	Mass number
A	14	28
B	13	27
C	15	31
D	12	26

12 Which atom (**A**, **B**, **C** or **D**) contains the most protons?

13 Three of these atoms contain the same number of neutrons. Which one (**A**, **B**, **C** or **D**) contains a different number of neutrons from the others?

14 Which compound does the formula $CuSO_4$ represent?

- **A** calcium sulphide
- **B** calcium sulphate
- **C** copper sulphide
- **D** copper sulphate

15 The diagram shows the structure of an atom.

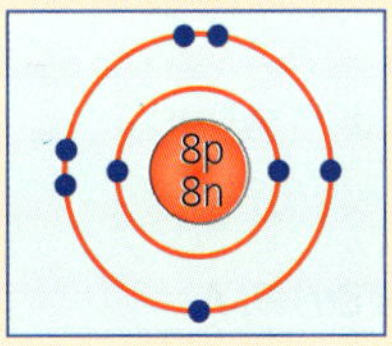

Which row of the table gives the correct atomic number and mass number for the atom?

	Atomic number	Mass number
A	8	8
B	8	16
C	16	8
D	16	16

16 Which row of the table shows a substance with ionic bonding?

	Melting point (°C)	Melting point (°C)
A	−10	60
B	800	2300
C	0	100
D	80	150

17 Ozone is a reactive form of oxygen. It has the formula O_3. An oxygen atom has an atomic number of 8 and a mass number of 16. The relative formula mass of ozone is:

- **A** 8
- **B** 16
- **C** 24
- **D** 48

Questions 18–20

The table gives information about protons, neutrons and electrons. It is not complete.

Particle	Charge	Relative mass
proton	+1	+1
electron		
neutron		+1

18 What is the relative formula mass of an electron?

- **A** negligible
- **B** +1
- **C** +2
- **D** −1

19 What is the relative charge on an electron?

- **A** −1
- **B** 0
- **C** +1
- **D** +2

20 What is the relative charge on a neutron?

- **A** −1
- **B** 0
- **C** +1
- **D** +2

Answers to these questions can be found on pages 140–144

Getting it right

1 (a) The diagram shows a water molecule.

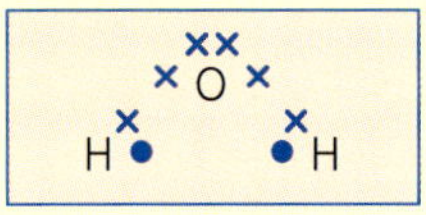

Complete the sentences below by using words from the list:

compound covalent ionic sharing

Water is a ______***compound***____ of two elements. The bonds in a water molecule are ___***covalent***___ bonds. Each bond involves the __***sharing***___ of a pair of electrons.

[3]

(b) Sodium chloride is a compound of two elements – sodium and chlorine.

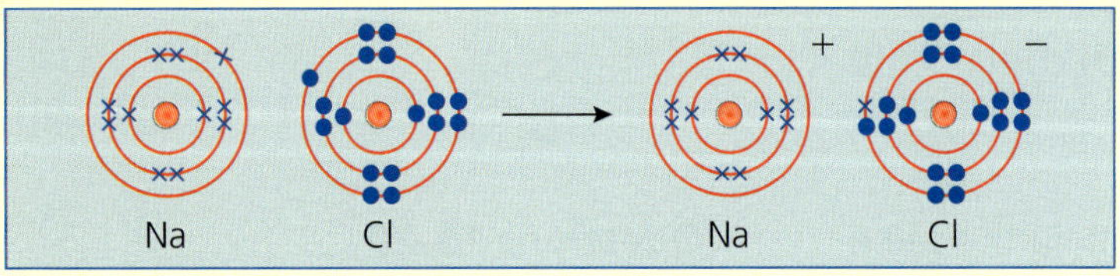

Use the diagram to explain how sodium and chlorine atoms combine to form sodium chloride.

Each sodium loses one electron; to form a sodium ion; each chlorine atom gans one electron; to form a chloride ion; opposite charges hold ions together. **[4]**

Ideas

There are three marks for any of the five marking points given. In addition there is a QWC mark that can be awarded if spelling, punctuation and grammar are accurate, so that the meaning is clear.

Transfer of electrons is an example given in the Specification where I and E can be covered.

2 Magnesium and oxygen combine to form magnesium oxide.

	Electron arrangement
Magnesium	2,8,2
Oxygen	2.6

(a) Describe the electronic changes that take place when magnesium and oxygen combine.

Magnesium atom loses two electrons; oxygen gains two electrons. **[2]**

(b) Calculate the relative formula mass of magnesium oxide. (Relative atomic masses: Mg = 24, O = 16)

Relative formula mass = 24 + 16 = 40 **[2]**

(c) When magnesium oxide is added to dilute hydrochloric acid, a reaction takes place. The temperature of the solution rises. What does this tell us about the reaction?

Reaction is exothermic. **[2]**

Movement and change

The first topic in this module considers how an object's motion depends on the forces acting on it. It includes a brief study of how our understanding of forces developed through the work of Galileo Galilei and Isaac Newton.

The second topic deals with energy and work and how they are related to each other and to power.

The two final topics are short. One is concerned with seismic waves and how changes in the geology of the Earth happen; the other examines the nature of radioactive decay. Knowledge about how radioactive materials decay is used to date rocks and other very old objects.

Forces and motion

You need to know

- how to interpret motion represented by graphs;
- know and use the relationship used to calculate acceleration;
- the factors that affect vehicle stopping distances;
- the history of the understanding of forces;
- how forces act between objects;
- how to describe the forces involved in free-fall motion;
- how the motion of an object in a straight line depends on the balance of the forces acting on it.

Speed, velocity and acceleration

You need to understand that

- The **speed** (in m/s) of an object is the distance (in m) that it travels each second (s).
- **Velocity** (in m/s) describes both the speed of an object and its direction of travel.

Speed is shown by the slope of a **distance–time graph**; the steeper the slope, the faster the speed.

A distance–time graph shows how the total distance travelled changes with time. Remember, the distance travelled can only increase, it can never decrease.

Speed can be calculated using the relationship:

speed = distance travelled ÷ time taken or $v = d/t$

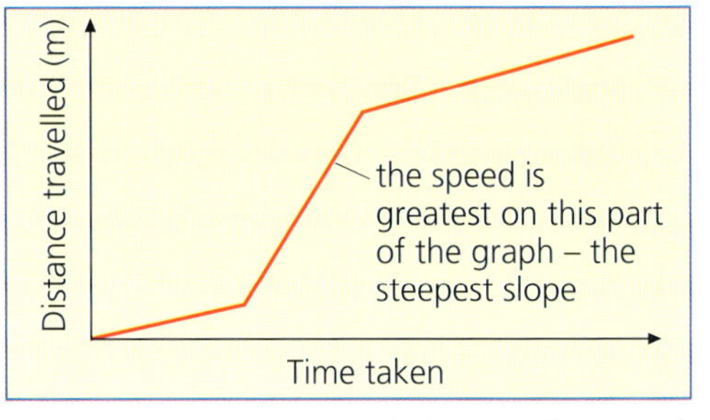

A distance–time graph

Another useful graph is a **speed–time graph**, which shows how the speed of an object changes. When the speed increases, the object is **accelerating**. The steeper the slope of the graph, the greater the acceleration. Acceleration means the increase in speed per second. A speed–time graph can be used to calculate acceleration by working out the slope.

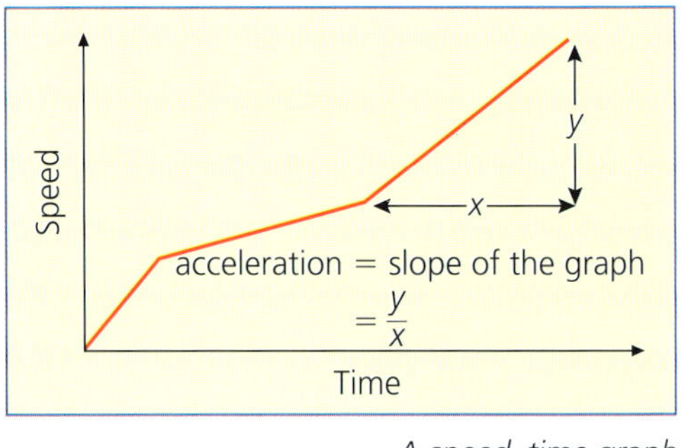

A speed–time graph

Stopping and starting

The total distance that the vehicle travels from when a hazard is seen to when the vehicle stops is called the **stopping distance**. It is made up of:

- **thinking distance** – the distance that the vehicle travels while the driver reacts;
- **braking distance** – the distance that the vehicle travels during braking.

Thinking distance depends on:

- The driver's reaction time – this is longer if the driver has taken drugs or alcohol or is being distracted.
- The speed of the vehicle – doubling the speed doubles the thinking distance.

Braking distance depends on:

- The mass of the vehicle – the greater the load, the greater the distance needed to brake.
- The speed of the vehicle – doubling the speed means that it travels four times the distance during braking.

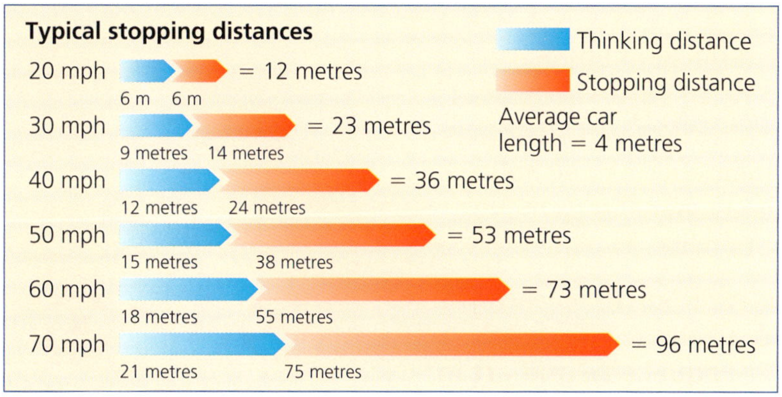

Keeping moving

It seemed obvious to the Greeks that to keep an object moving, you need to keep pushing or pulling it. However, they were not aware of the "unseen" forces of:

- **friction** – a force that acts against solid objects slipping and sliding over each other;
- **air resistance** – a force that acts against motion through the air.

When you move through a fluid such as air or water, you have to push the fluid out of the way to make room for your body. The force acting against your motion is air resistance or water resistance.

Falling down

Two forces act on an object that is falling through the air:

- the Earth's gravitational pull acts downwards – this force is the object's weight;
- air resistance pushes upwards – the size of this force depends on the shape of the object and its speed.

As an object falls, the balance of the forces acting on it changes.

At low speeds there is little air resistance and the weight of the object causes it to accelerate downwards. As it speeds up, the air resistance increases. The acceleration becomes

continued →

smaller. When the air resistance is equal in size to the object's weight, the forces are balanced. The object now travels at a constant speed called the **terminal velocity.**

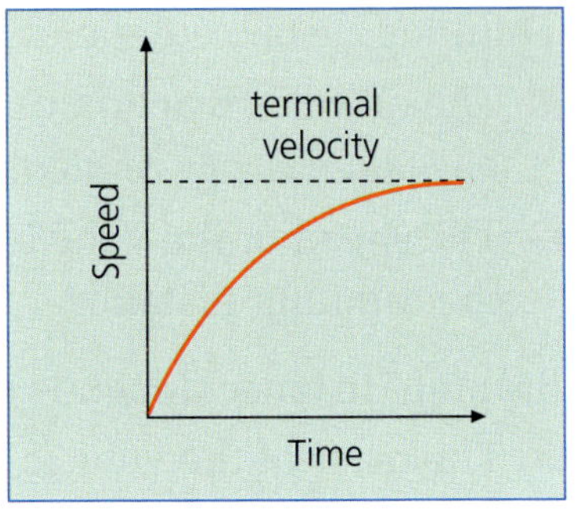

On the Moon

Things are very different on the Moon. Because there is no atmosphere, there is no air resistance, and all objects fall at the same rate with the same acceleration.

Back to Earth

Things fall downwards because of the gravitational attraction between them and the Earth. Newton realised that gravitational attractive forces act between all objects but they are often too small for their effects to be noticed. The forces are only large enough to make things move when one of the objects has a lot of mass, as planets have.

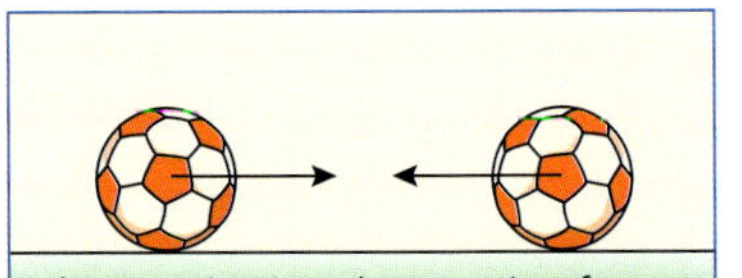
the gravitational attractive force between these two balls is tiny, so they do not move together

Newton also realised that objects exert forces on each other. This means that if you kick a ball the force on the foot and the force on the ball are of **equal size and act in opposite directions**. The forces also have different effects because they act on objects of different mass. The ball has a small mass and so it gains a large forward-directed acceleration. The large mass of the person means that they gain only a small acceleration in a backwards direction.

Both Galileo and Newton realised that if an object is not moving or is moving in a straight line at a constant speed then the forces on it are **balanced**. If the forces are balanced, equal forces act in opposite directions to cancel each other out. If the forces on an object are **unbalanced**, it accelerates in the direction of the greater force.

Questions

1. What is "thinking distance"?
2. An object is falling at a constant speed through the Earth's atmosphere. What is this speed called?
3. A car speeds up from 15 m/s to 30 m/s in 12 s. Calculate its acceleration.

Forces and energy

You need to know

- ✔ the relationship for calculating work and how to use it;
- ✔ how to recognise situations where objects have kinetic energy and gravitational potential energy;
- ✔ that work and energy transfer are equivalent;
- ✔ the relationship for calculating power.

Working

When you lift something up or push something along, you are working. **Work** is being done when a force makes something move.

Work is measured in joules (J) and the amount of work done can be calculated using the relationship:

work done = force × distance moved or $W = F \times d$

You are working even when you are sat perfectly still, because the cells in your body are respiring and your heart is pumping blood around your body.

Work and energy

To be able to do work, you need **energy**. As you work, energy flows from you to the object being moved.

Two important ways in which objects can gain energy are:

- through movement – a moving object can do work and is said to have **kinetic energy**;
- through position – an object that has been lifted up stores energy as **gravitational potential energy**.

Doing work and transferring energy mean the same thing.

A moving ball or vehicle has kinetic energy. Energy stored in the weight of a grandfather clock is gravitational potential energy.

How powerful?

Power describes the amount of work done or energy transferred each second. It is calculated using the relationship:

power = work done ÷ time taken or $P = W \div t$

Power is measured in watts (W), where one watt is equivalent to one joule per second, 1 W = 1 J/s.

Take care with the use of the word "power" in tests and exams. In everyday chat it is often used to mean "force" rather than "rate of energy transfer".

Questions

1. What type of energy does a person gain when climbing stairs?
2. A man uses a force of 30 N to push a supermarket trolley 150 m. How much work does he do?
3. A ball is thrown up into the air. What energy transfer takes place immediately after it leaves the hand?

Earth waves

You need to know

- ✔ how to describe the structure of the lithosphere in terms of plates;
- ✔ that earthquakes are caused when plates slide past each other;
- ✔ how rock is recycled by plates moving towards and away from each other.

Waves that travel through the body or along the surface of the Earth are called **seismic waves**. They can be caused by earthquakes or by an explosion occurring underground.

The detection of seismic waves provides information about changes taking place in the structure of the Earth.

The outer layer of the solid part of the Earth is called the **lithosphere**. The diagram shows how it is made up of several sections called **plates**. Convection currents inside the Earth cause the plates to move.

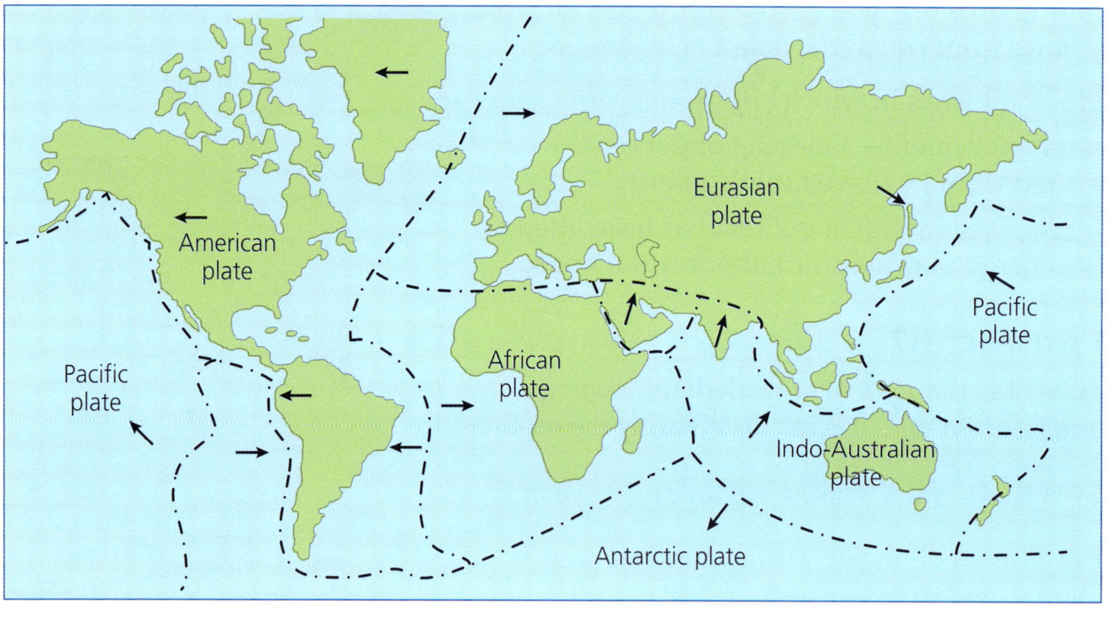

The plates that make up the surface of the Earth

The moving plates can:

- slide past each other – an earthquake is caused when there is a sudden "jolt";
- move towards each other – this can result in the formation of mountain ranges;
- move away from each other – this causes volcanoes.

When plates move towards each other, the ocean floor plate is forced under the continental crust plate. Rock from the ocean floor plate is heated and melts in the Earth's **magma**, the hot molten rock in the mantle underneath the Earth's crust.

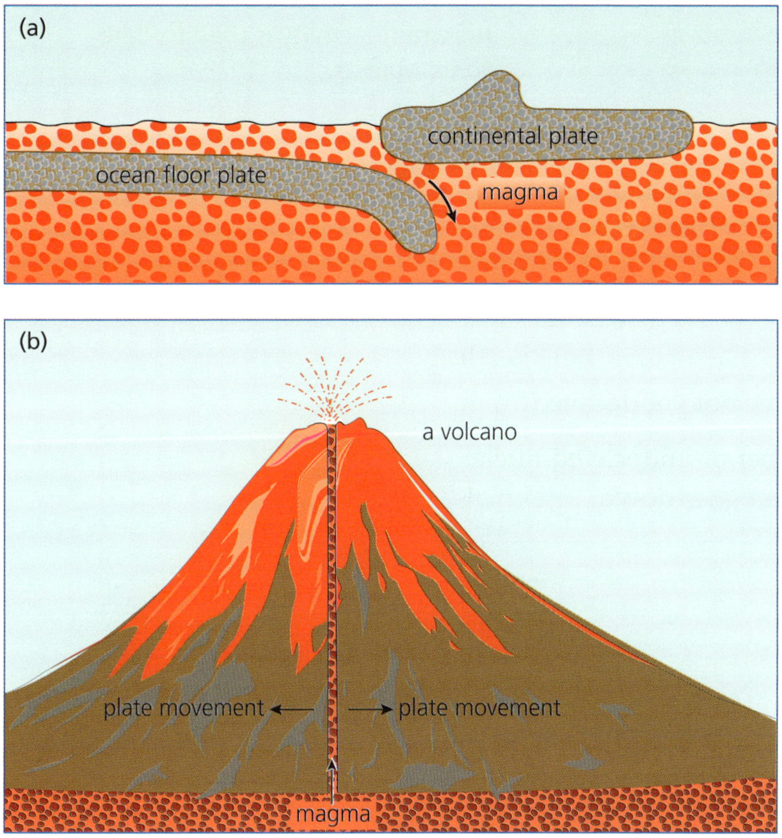

Plates moving (a) towards each other, (b) away from each other

When plates move away from each other, molten rock from the magma escapes from the gap between them. This magma cools and solidifies to form new rock. If this occurs on dry land it forms a volcano.

Questions

1. What name is given to waves that travel through the body of the Earth?
2. When an ocean floor plate slides under a continental plate, what happens to the rock?
3. What type of plate movement causes a volcano?

Using half-life

You need to know

- how the decay of radioactive isotope changes over time;
- the meaning of half-life
- about the problems in disposing of radioactive waste;
- how radioactivity is used to date some objects.

Some isotopes are stable – others are unstable. The radioactive decay of an isotope is measured in **becquerels** (Bq), where 1 Bq = 1 decay per second. This decay rate depends on:

- the isotope;
- the number of nuclei that have not yet decayed.

As the isotope decays, the number of undecayed nuclei goes down, so the decay rate also goes down.

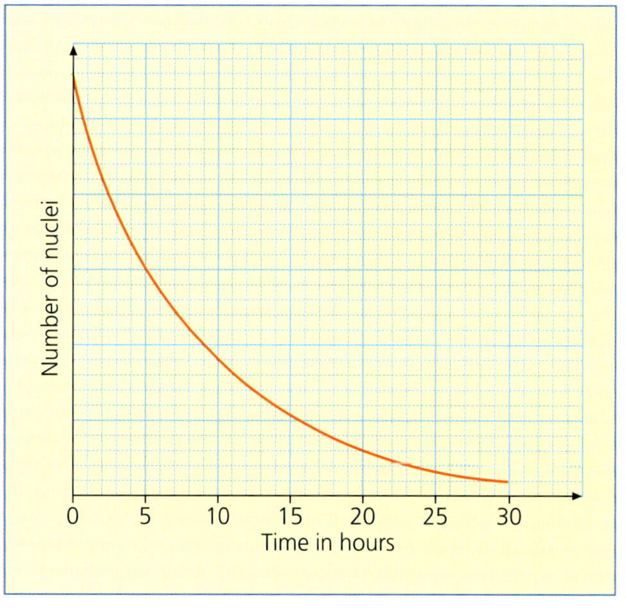

No matter what the time-scale, all radioactive decay follows the pattern shown in the graph.

For the isotope shown in the graph, the number of remaining, undecayed nuclei halves every 6 hours. This time is called the **half-life** of the isotope.

After one half-life, the decay rate also halves.

Some isotopes have much longer half-lives and some have much shorter ones, but they all show the same pattern of decay.

Radioactive dating

Whatever the number of nuclei of a radioactive isotope present in a sample of radioactive material, half of them decay during each half-life. This means that:

- after one half-life has passed, half of the nuclei are undecayed;
- after two half-lives have passed, half of these undecayed nuclei have decayed, leaving just a quarter of the original nuclei undecayed;
- after three half-lives have passed, only half of these are undecayed – note that all of those remaining are undecayed, so just one-eighth of the original nuclei remain undecayed.

A common wrong idea at GCSE is that after two half-lives "all the nuclei have died". Nuclei do not die, they decay. After two half-lives, one-quarter of them are undecayed.

Measuring the number of nuclei of an isotope present in an object can be used to estimate its age:

- Living things absorb small amounts of radioactive carbon-14 from the air and their food. When a living thing dies, the amount of radioactive carbon-14 that it contains decays with a half-life of 6000 years. Measuring the amount of carbon-14 remaining enables the date of death to be estimated.
- Rocks contain radioactive isotopes. The fewer the nuclei of these isotopes present in a rock, the greater its age.

Radiocarbon dating is a useful technique for dating old timber and archaeological samples.

Radioactive dating of rocks has been used to estimate the age of the Earth and the Moon.

Knowing the half-life of radioactive materials also helps in deciding how to dispose of radioactive waste. Waste must be stored until ten half-lives have passed for it to be "safe".

For some isotopes used in medicine this takes only a few days, but for some waste materials from nuclear power stations this can take thousands of years.

Questions

1 As a radioactive isotope decays, what happens to the number of nuclei of the isotope?

2 A radioactive isotope has a half-life of 6 hours. Its rate of decay is measured to be 1200 Bq. Calculate the rate of decay (a) after 6 hours; (b) after a further 6 hours.

3 Which of the following can be dated using radiocarbon dating?

cloth   pottery   wood

Practice module test

You will have 20 minutes to answer these questions

The distance–time graph represents a race between four cyclists.

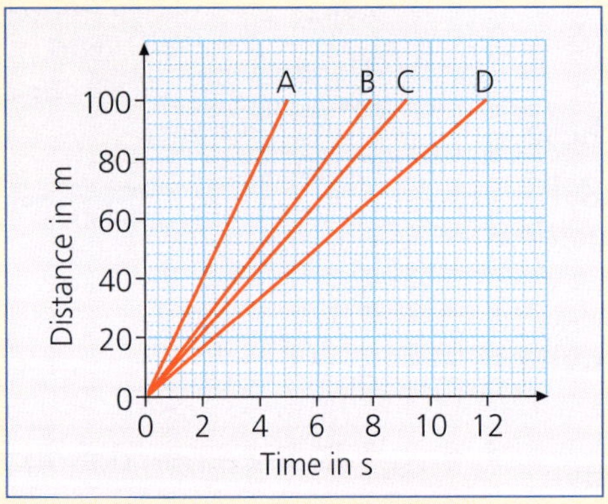

1 Which cyclist lost the race?

2 Which cyclist had a speed of 12.5 m/s?

3 The speed of cyclist A was

A 10 m/s
B 20 m/s
C 80 m/s
D 100 m/s

4 Which of these could increase a driver's reaction time?

A alertness
B breathing
C respiring
D tiredness

5 The diagram shows the forces between the Earth and the Moon. The forces are:

A electrical
B gravitational
C frictional
D magnetic

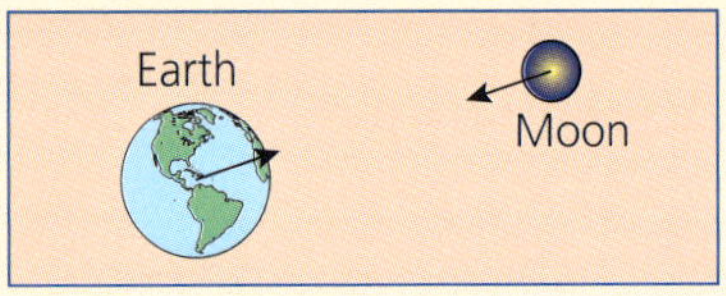

6 If a feather and a coin are released together above the surface of the Moon:

A the feather has the greater acceleration
B the coin has the greater acceleration
C they have the same acceleration
D they do not accelerate

7 Kinetic energy is energy that is:

A a result of movement
B a result of position
C potential
D stored

8 A girl does 1000 J of work. She loses:

A no energy
B less than 1000 J of energy
C 1000 J of energy
D more than 1000 J of energy

9 A boy can increase his gravitational potential energy by:

A moving uphill
B moving downhill
C running
D standing still

10 Earthquakes cause:

A light waves
B plate waves
C seismic waves
D tectonic waves

11 New rock is formed when tectonic plates:

A move away from each other
B move over and under each other
C move towards each other
D slide past each other

12 Radiocarbon dating can be used to date archaeological specimens that:

- **A** are alive
- **B** never lived
- **C** absorb radio waves
- **D** were once alive

13 Velocity describes:

- **A** speed and its unit
- **B** speed upwards
- **C** speed downwards
- **D** speed and direction

Questions 14–17

The diagram show the horizontal forces acting on a car.

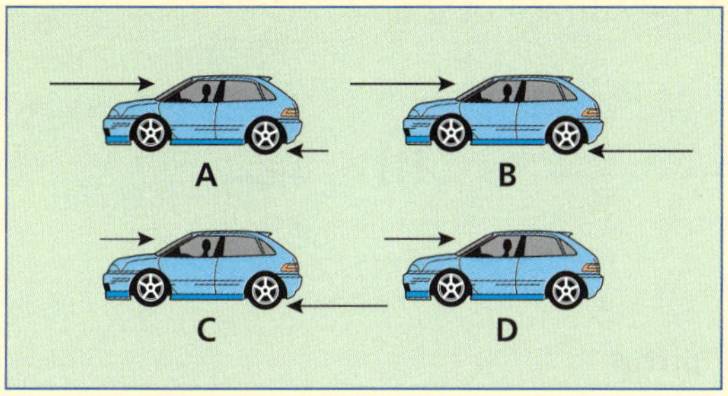

14 Which car is accelerating forwards?

15 Which car has balanced forces acting on it?

16 Which car could be braking?

17 Which car is travelling at a constant speed?

18 A car speeds up from 12 m/s to 16 m/s in 2.0 s. Its acceleration is:

- **A** 0.5 m/s
- **B** 0.5 m/s^2
- **C** 2.0 m/s
- **D** 2.0 m/s^2

19 Power means:

- **A** the size of a force
- **B** the strength of a force
- **C** how much work is done
- **D** the work done by a force per second

20 When a weightlifter lifts some weights, the weights gain:

- **A** gravitational potential energy
- **B** kinetic energy
- **C** movement energy
- **D** thermal energy

21 The outermost layer of the solid Earth is called:

- **A** the duosphere
- **B** the ionosphere
- **C** the lithosphere
- **D** the monosphere

22 When an ocean plate moves under a continental plate, rocks are:

- **A** melted in the Earth's inner core
- **B** melted in the Earth's outer core
- **C** melted in the Earth's crust
- **D** melted in the Earth's mantle

23 The half-life of a radioactive isotope:

- **A** increases with increasing time
- **B** decreases with increasing time
- **C** has a constant value
- **D** is half of the dead-life

24 A radioactive isotope has a half-life of 60 s. The decay rate is measured to be 120 Bq. 120 s later the decay rate is likely to be:

- **A** 30 Bq
- **B** 60 Bq
- **C** 240 Bq
- **D** 480 Bq

Answers to these questions can be found on pages 140–144

Getting it right

An astronaut drops a piece of Moon rock. The graph shows how the speed of the rock changes from when it leaves the astronaut's hand to when it reaches the Moon's surface.

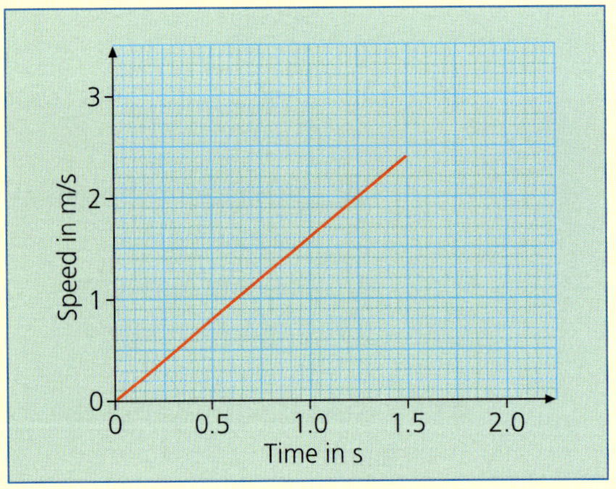

(a) What was the speed of the rock as it reached the surface of the Moon?

2.4 m/s **[1]**

This question is testing your skills at handling data; in this case, interpreting the graph scale.

(b) Calculate the acceleration of the rock.

Acceleration = increase in speed ÷ time
= 2.4 m/s ÷ 1.5 s
= 1.6 m/s^2 **[3]**

(c) When a similar rock dropped above the surface of the Earth, its acceleration was greater. Explain why.

The Earth's gravitational field is stronger, so there is a greater unbalanced force on the mass. **[2]**

Remember, the cue word "explain" means that you need to give a reason. In this case the reason for the greater force is the increased gravitational field strength.

(d) When Galileo dropped two masses from the top of the leaning tower of Pisa, the heavier mass reached the ground a fraction of a second before the lighter one. Some people claimed that this proved that heavier objects fall faster than lighter ones. Suggest an alternative explanation.

The masses were affected by air resistance. This had a greater effect on the lighter mass than on the heavier one. **[2]**

One key aspect of the assessment of "ideas and evidence" is whether you understand that experimental evidence can be interpreted in different ways.

Energy, communication and force

The major topic in this module talks about using electricity to transfer energy. It starts with a study of electrostatics and then links that to current in circuits. This is followed by a study of the generation and transmission of electricity.

The communication topic covers wave behaviour and how this is used in effective communications. The final topic is concerned with how forces change the size, shape and volume of materials.

Charge and energy

You need to know

- how an insulator can be charged;
- how to describe the forces between charged objects;
- how to describe some uses of electrostatic charge;
- how to describe some dangers of electrostatic charge.

Charging and discharging

Metals are electrical **conductors** – they allow charge to flow through them. Non-metals do not allow charge to pass through – they are **insulators**. When charge is placed on an insulator, it stays there. This is known as an **electrostatic charge**, because it does not move through the insulator.

You can easily charge insulators such as plastics, for example by rubbing them with a duster. This results in the transfer of negatively charged **electrons**. The object that gains electrons becomes negatively charged. The object that loses electrons becomes positively charged.

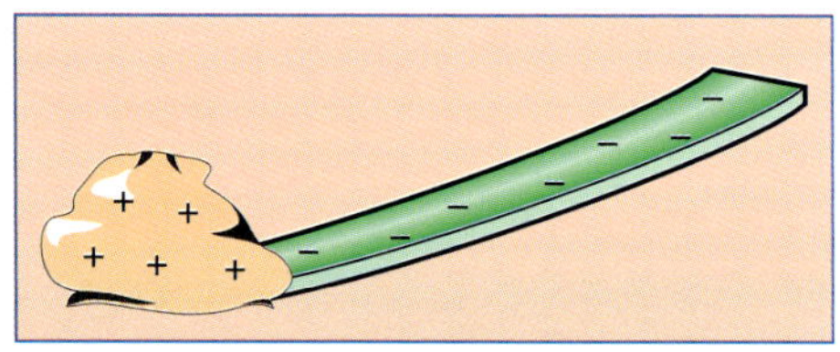

Charging a polythene rod with a duster

The balloons in the diagram are held apart by electrostatic forces. The forces are repulsive because both balloons have the same type of charge.

Charged objects exert electrical forces on each other – like charges repel and unlike charges attract.

A large build-up of charge can create a high voltage, big enough to make the air conduct electricity. This is what happens when lightning occurs – the high voltage between the bottom of a cloud and the ground splits the air up into positive and negative ions. Movement of these ions results in a flash of lightning and discharges the cloud.

When answering questions about electrostatic charge, always use this rule to give the reason for your answer.

Movement of charge can also cause unpleasant shocks:

- Synthetic fabrics such as nylon and polyester are very good electrical insulators.
- If you sit on a car seat or walk across a nylon carpet while wearing these fabrics, you become charged.
- Touching a car door or an earthed object such as the screw of a light switch causes you to discharge as electrons move between you and the Earth.
- The result is that you feel a shock as charge flows through you.

Because these materials are good electrical insulators, charge cannot pass through them to earth.

Electrostatic charge can be both dangerous and useful, depending on the circumstances:

- when cars and aircraft are being refuelled, charge can build up on the metal bodywork;
- a spark could cause the fuel to ignite.

To avoid this hazard:

- The body of an aircraft is always connected to the ground while it is being refuelled. This provides a safe route for the charge to pass through.
- The fuel pipe of a car is connected to the metal car body so that the charge spreads out and a high voltage does not build up.

If the aircraft is connected to the earth, there can be no voltage between them to cause a spark.

Electric charge is useful:

- in photocopiers, where the black powder only sticks to charged areas of the belt;
- in inkjet printers, where the motion of the drops is controlled by charged metal plates.

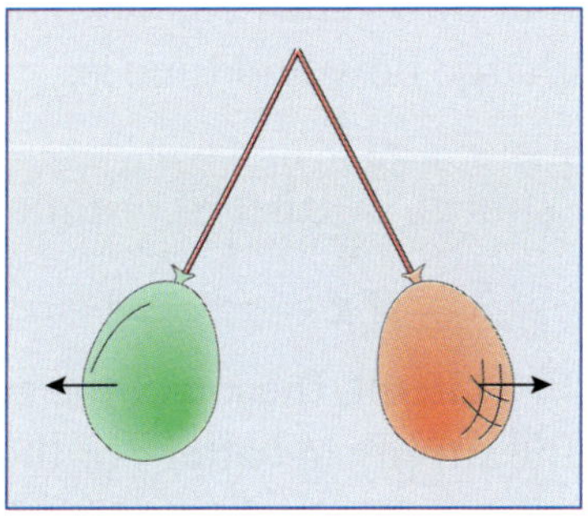

Both balloons have the same type of charge

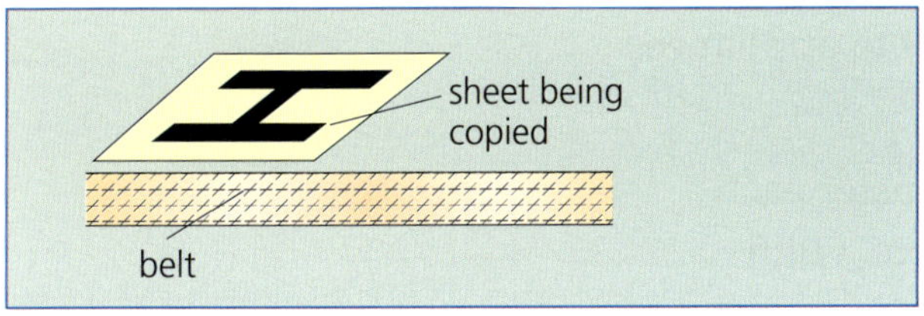

A photocopier uses black powder on a belt to make a print. Where light passes through the sheet being copied, the belt discharges and does not attract the black powder

Questions

1 Which words from the list describe the forces between two positively charged balloons?

attractive electrostatic gravitational magnetic repulsive

2 A balloon is charged with a duster. Electrons move from the duster to the balloon. What type of charge is gained by:

a the balloon? **b** the duster?

3 How does earthing an aircraft prevent an explosion during refuelling?

Charge and current

You need to know

- ✔ the relationship between current and charge flow;
- ✔ the relationship between power, current and voltage;
- ✔ how to explain the principles of a motor and a transformer;
- ✔ how transformers are used in transmitting electricity.

Electric **charge**, Q, is measured in **coulombs** (C).
Any flow of electric charge is a **current**. The size of the current is equal to the rate of charge flow, or the current that flows each second. The relationship between current, charge flow and time is:

charge = current × time or $Q = I \times t$

In a circuit, the job of the current is to transfer energy from the supply (a battery or the mains electricity) to appliances such as lamps, heaters and motors.

The rate of energy transfer, or the energy transfer each second, is the power supplied to the appliance. High-powered appliances such as heaters need a large current to transfer the energy required each second. The relationship between current, power and voltage is:

power = current × voltage or $P = I \times V$

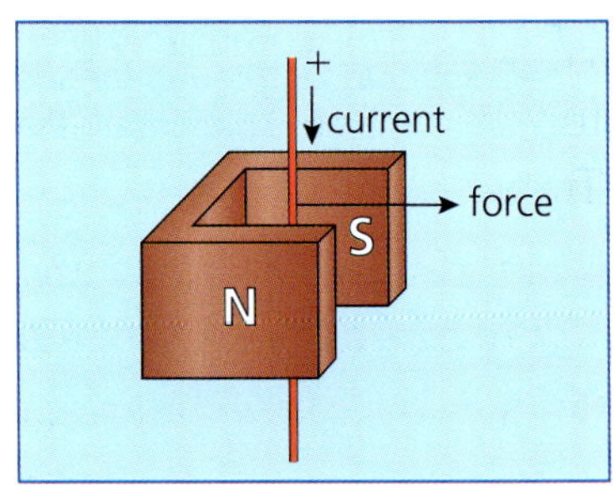

The force on a wire carrying a current

Motors and transformers

Electric **motors** use energy from the electricity supply to produce movement. They rely on the fact that:

- if there is a current in a wire placed at right angles to the direction of a magnetic field, there is a force on the wire;
- the direction of the force is at right angles to both the current and the magnetic field;
- reversing the current reverses the direction of the force.

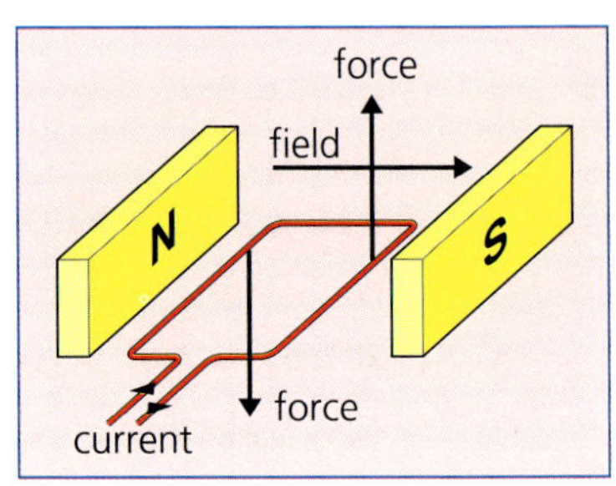

The forces on the wire loop cause it to turn anticlockwise

A **transformer** is a device that changes the size of an alternating voltage. It is made of two coils of wire wound on the same iron core.

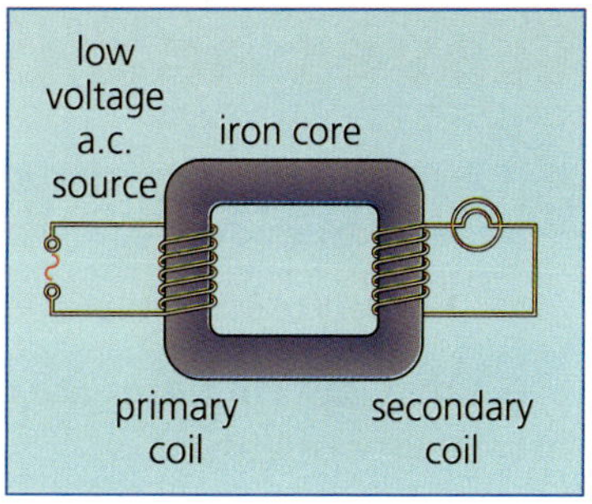

The structure of a transformer

The output voltage from the transformer:

- is greater than the input voltage if the secondary coil has more turns than the primary – this is called a step-up transformer;
- is less than the input voltage if the secondary coil has fewer turns than the primary – this is called a step-down transformer.

Delivering power

Electricity is transmitted from power stations to homes and workplaces through a system of cables called the National Grid. Some of these cables are underground and some are overhead, supported by pylons. The cables become heated by the current passing through them. This wastes energy from the electricity supply.

To reduce the amount of energy wasted, the current needs to be as small as possible. This means that the voltage has to be large, so that the required amount of power is transmitted.

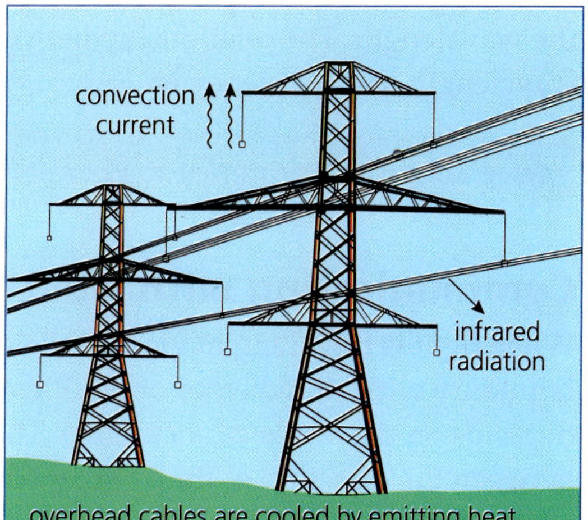

overhead cables are cooled by emitting heat to their surroundings

The National Grid carries electricity at voltages up to 400 000 V. This would be far too dangerous for householders to use. Transformers are used to:

- increase the voltage and reduce the current at the power station;
- decrease the voltage and increase the current at a substation near to your house.

Questions

1. What is the relationship between moving charge and the size of an electric current?
2. The current in a 240 V mains kettle is 9.5 A. Calculate the power of the kettle.
3. Explain why high voltages are used to transmit electricity.
4. What device is used to increase the voltage generated at the power station?

Waves and communication

You need to know

- how to use the wave equation;
- how optical fibres are used in communication;
- how to describe diffraction effects and recall the factors that affect the amount of diffraction that takes place.

Wave properties

Waves are used to transfer energy and information.

When waves travel from one place to another, they may cause particles to vibrate, but there is no overall movement of particles between the two places.

When waves transfer energy from one place to another, there is no overall movement of any material. It is only the vibrations that move.

The speed of a wave depends on the type of wave it is and what it is travelling through. Electromagnetic waves such as light and radio waves travel much faster than compression waves such as sound.

For all types of wave, the higher the frequency, the shorter the wavelength. The relationship between speed, wavelength and frequency is:

wave speed = frequency × wavelength or $v = f \times \lambda$

You need to know and be able to use this relationship to answer questions in modular tests and written examinations.

Communicating with waves

When light is travelling in glass or water and it meets a boundary with air, whether or not it crosses the boundary depends on the **angle of incidence**. This is the angle between the direction of the light and a line drawn at right angles to the surface.

- At low angles of incidence, some light is reflected and some crosses the boundary.
- At the **critical angle of incidence** the light that escapes forms a spectrum along the boundary.
- At angles of incidence greater than the critical angle, all the light is reflected – this is known as **total internal reflection**.

The critical angle for a glass–air boundary is 42°, so light incident at an angle of 45° is totally internally reflected.

Total internal reflection is used to turn light round corners in **reflecting prisms** and to contain light within an **optical fibre** so that information can be transmitted over long distances.

All communications are affected by **diffraction**. This describes the way in which waves spread out when they pass through a gap:

- if the size of the gap is many wavelengths (diagram a), no observable spreading occurs;
- if the gap is several wavelengths wide (diagram b), there is some spreading into the "shadow" region;
- if the size of the gap is equal to the wavelength (diagram c), the waves spread so that they can be detected in all directions.

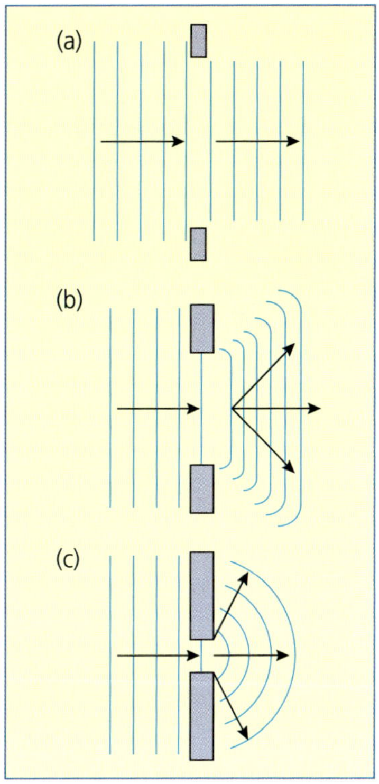

Common effects of diffraction include:

- Sound spreads out as it passes through a doorway – the size of the gap is comparable to the wavelength.
- Light does not spread out as it passes through a doorway – the size of the gap is millions of wavelengths of light. Instead, light travels in straight lines and forms shadows.
- Water waves spread out as they pass through the entrance into a harbour.

Radio and television reception are affected by both diffraction and reflection. Diffraction causes long wavelength radio waves to spread out as they pass over hills and through gaps between buildings so that they can be received in "shadow regions".

The waves that carry television signals and FM radio have a much shorter wavelength. They show very little spreading as they pass round obstacles and through gaps, so reception in hilly areas and cities can be poor.

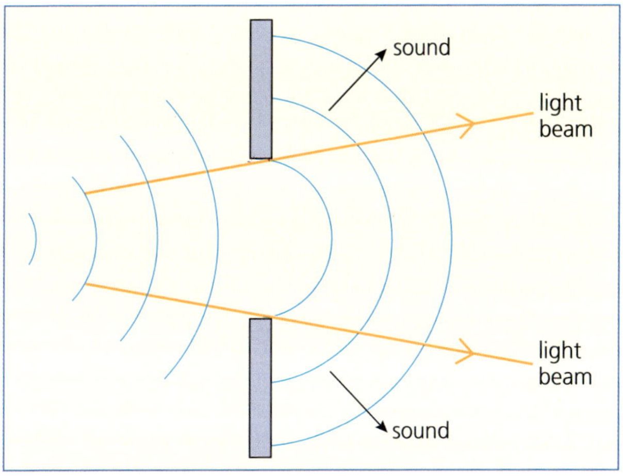

Light travels in straight lines through a doorway but sound spreads out – this shows how diffraction depends on the wavelength of the waves

Questions

1. Calculate the speed of a wave that has a frequency of 500 Hz and a wavelength of 2.6 m.
2. What is the condition needed for total internal reflection to take place when light meets a glass–air surface?
3. Explain why light travels as a straight beam after passing through a gap that is 5 mm wide but sound spreads out.

Forces and shape

You need to know

- ✔ how the forces from the supports of a bridge change with the position of the load;
- ✔ how to describe how the extension of a rubber band or spring depends on the stretching force;
- ✔ how gas pressure is caused by particle movement.

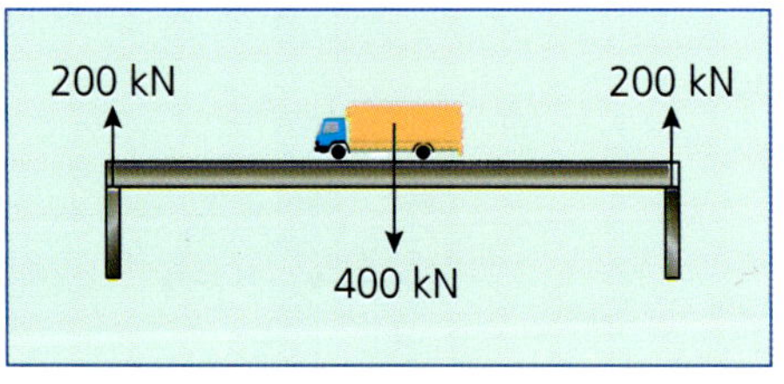

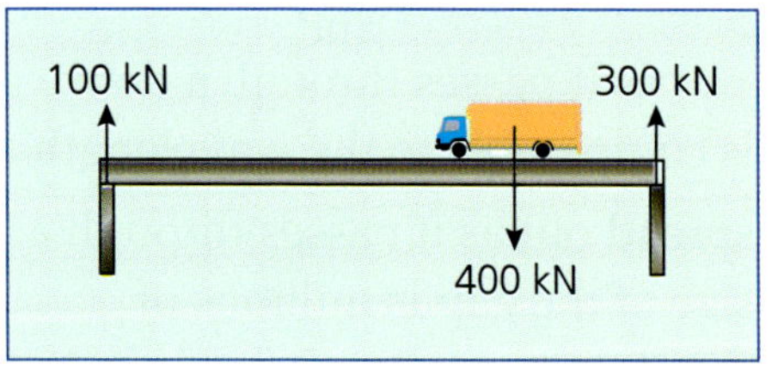

A simple road bridge consists of a horizontal beam that is supported by two upright concrete pillars. The pillars have to support the weight of the beam as well as any traffic on it. To do this, they exert an upward push on the beam. The greater the load, the greater this push has to be. The two diagrams show the additional forces that act on the bridge because of the weight of the lorry.

When a load such as a lorry is in the centre of the bridge, the upward forces from the pillars are equal. The nearer the lorry is to one end of the bridge, the greater the upward push from that support.

All materials change shape when they are pulled or pushed. Springs, rubber bands and some wires stretch by a large and measurable amount. The diagrams compare the stretching of these materials.

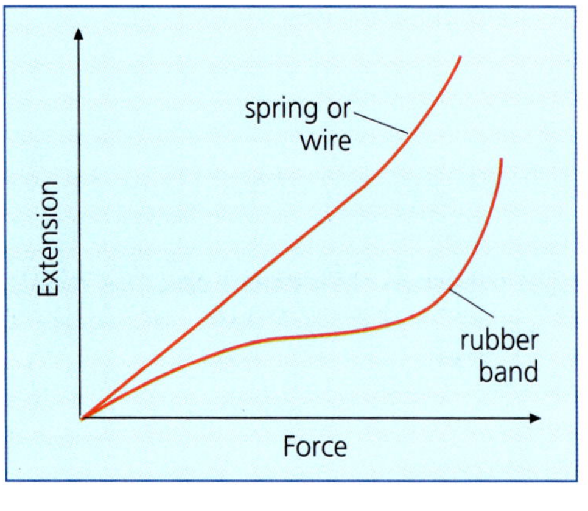

Springs and metal wires behave in a similar way:

- At first the extension is proportional to the force – shown by the straight line part of the graph.
- After this they become easier to stretch but do not return to their original size when the force is removed.

Rubber bands behave differently:

- There is no linear part to the extension–force graph.
- They are difficult to stretch at first, becoming easier to stretch as the force is increased and then more difficult.

Gases consist of large numbers of particles in continual motion. This motion is both rapid and random:

- the particles move at high speeds (on average);
- the speed and direction of any one particle is unpredictable and continually changing.

The motion of gas particles explains how they exert pressure:

- the particles hit the container walls and rebound;
- each collision causes a pushing force on the wall.

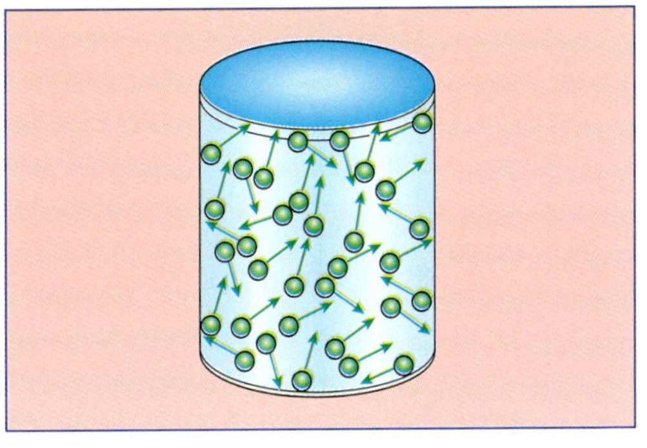

The motion of gas particles is random in both speed and direction

Pressure results from the overall effect of millions of collisions with the container walls each second.

Questions

1 A spring stretches by 10 cm when a 20 N force is applied. (a) How much does it stretch when a 5 N force is applied? (b) What have you assumed about the spring?

2 How does a gas exert pressure?

Practice module test

You will have 20 minutes to answer these questions

1 Two objects with the same type of charge:

A attract each other
B deflect each other
C detract each other
D repel each other

2 Which of the following is an electrical insulator?

A copper
B iron
C plastic
D steel

3 A metal object can only hold static charge if it is:

A connected to the air
B insulated from the air
C connected to the ground
D insulated from the ground

4 The force on a conducting wire in a magnetic field is used in a:

A motor
B photocopier
C pylon
D transformer

5 A transformer can be used to:

A make a direct voltage bigger
B make a direct voltage smaller
C change an alternating voltage into a direct one
D make an alternating voltage smaller

6 Lightning is caused by the movement of:

A charge
B current
C voltage
D power

7 Which letter shows a possible direction of the force on the wire?

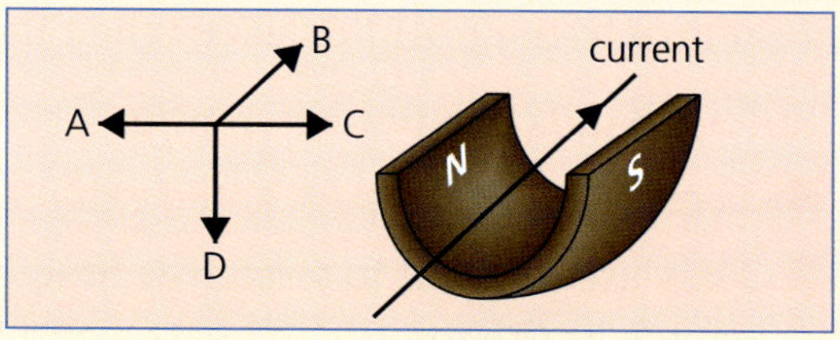

8 Which diagram shows total internal reflection by a prism?

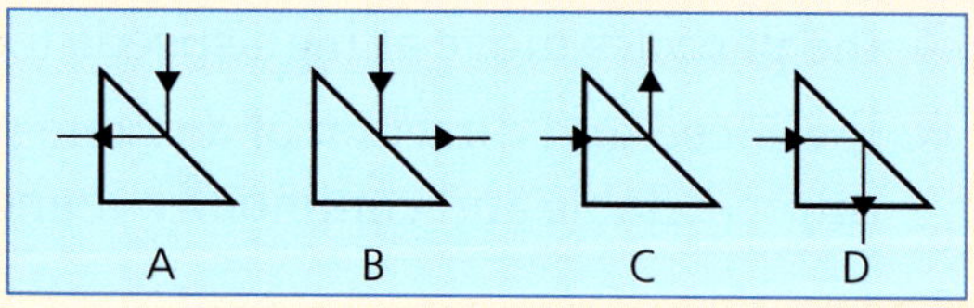

9 Waves always transfer:

A energy
B information
C mass
D matter

10 Total internal reflection is used to transfer energy in:

A motors
B optical fibres
C transformers
D windows

11 The graph shows how the extension changes with force for:

A copper wire
B steel wire
C a steel spring
D a rubber band

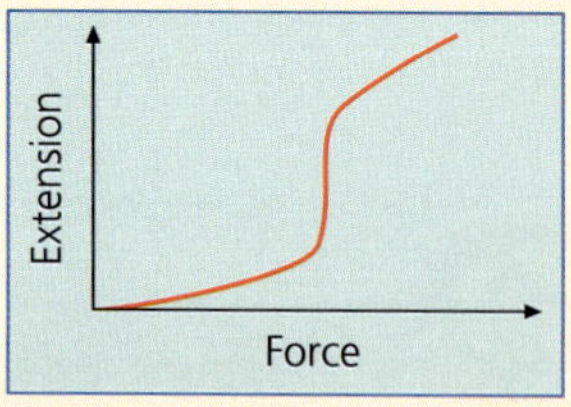

12 The particles of a gas:

A do not move
B move in an orderly way
C move at the same speed
D have a range of speeds

13 The current in a lamp filament is 2.0 A when it operates from a 12 V battery. The charge flow through the lamp in one minute is:

A 6 C
B 24 C
C 120 C
D 1440 C

14 Which particles are transferred when a balloon is rubbed with a duster?

A negatively-charged electrons
B positively-charged electrons
C negatively-charged protons
D positively-charged protons

15 In an inkjet printer, charged plates are used to:

A colour the ink drops
B deflect the ink drops
C disperse the ink drops
D reflect the ink drops

16 The current in a toaster element is 5.0 A when it operates from the 240 V mains supply. The power of the element is:

A 48 C
B 48 W
C 1200 C
D 1200 W

17 Which line in the table shows the action of a step-up transformer?

	Input voltage	Output voltage
A	12 V d.c.	240 V d.c.
B	240 V d.c.	12 V d.c.
C	12 V a.c	240 V a.c.
D	240 V a.c	12 V a.c.

18 Electricity is transmitted at high voltage to reduce the energy lost as:

A current
B heat
C power
D voltage

19 Diffraction effects are shown by:

A light but not sound
B sound but not light
C neither light nor sound
D both light and sound

20 Which diagram shows waves being diffracted?

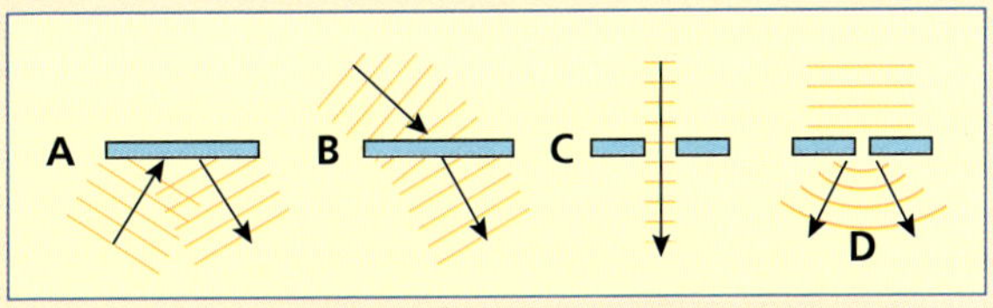

21 A "ghost" image on a television screen is caused by:

A diffraction
B interference
C reflection
D refraction

22 Total internal reflection occurs when:

A the angle of incidence is less than the critical angle
B the angle of incidence is greater than the critical angle
C the angle of reflection is less than the critical angle
D the angle of reflection is greater than the critical angle

23 Gas pressure is a result of:

A the particles being squashed together
B the particles being widespread
C the particles colliding with each other
D the particles colliding with the walls of the container

24 The movement of the particles in a gas is:

A random
B seldom
C often
D frequent

Answers to these questions can be found on pages 140–144

Getting it right

(a) The diagram shows a balloon and a duster, after the balloon has been rubbed with the duster.

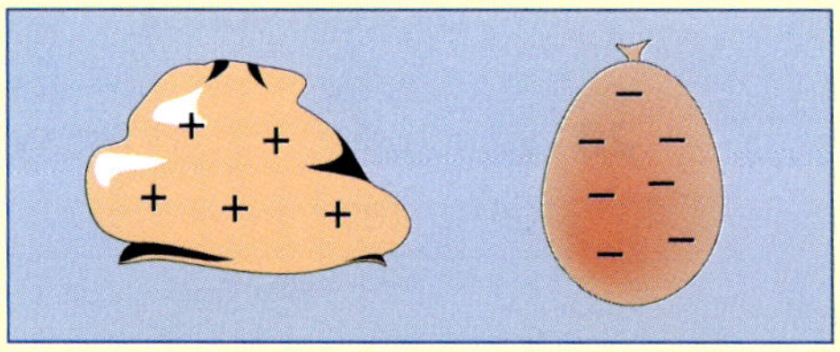

(i) What type of force exists between the balloon and the duster? Give reasons for your answer.

The force is attractive. The balloon and duster have opposite charges and opposite charges attract. **[3]**

(ii) Explain how the balloon and the duster become charged

Electrons move from the duster to the balloon. **[2]**

Always give full reasons when told to do so. Candidates often lose marks by leaving the examiner to infer part of the answer

(b) When an aircraft is being refuelled, charge can build up on the metal body of the aircraft.

(i) Explain how the whole of the body of the aircraft becomes charged.

The metal body conducts electricity. Charge can move through a conductor. **[2]**

(ii) Suggest why this build-up of charge could be dangerous. Give reasons for your answer.

The charge could create a high voltage. This could cause a spark, which could ignite the fuel. **[3]**

The extra mark here is given for the quality of written communication. The answer is clear and logical, with correct punctuation and grammar. You can recognise where marks are awarded for the quality of written communication by the icon in the margin.

Exam questions

Question 1B

The diagram shows structures involved in sweating.

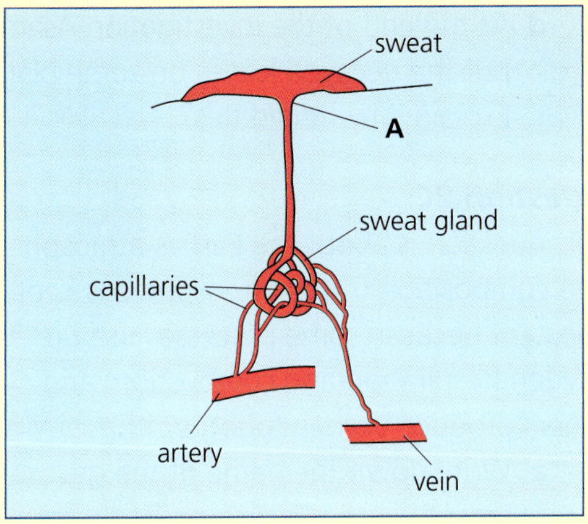

a Name part A. [1]

b Sweat is shown on the surface of the skin.

i Name two substances contained in sweat. [2]

ii How do substances in sweat reach the sweat gland? [1]

iii Explain how the sweat cools the body down. [3]

c Antiperspirant sprays stop you sweating from the skin that they cover. What effect does this have on body temperature? [1]

d Explain how the skin prevents entry of harmful microorganisms into the body. [3]

Question 1C

a Atoms of elements are made up from three particles – electrons, protons and neutrons. Which particles are present in the nucleus of a carbon atom? [1]

b The table below gives the symbols of the elements in Period 3 of the periodic table. Use only these elements in your answers.

Group no.	1	2	3	4	5	6	7	8
	Na	Mg	Al	Si	P	S	Cl	Ar

i Write down the symbols for two metallic elements. [2]

ii Write down the symbol for a noble gas. [1]

iii Sodium and chlorine react together to form a compound. Write down the name of the compound. [1]

iv The atomic number of Na is 11. What is the atomic number of P? [1]

v Atoms of these elements have different numbers of electrons in their outer shells. Describe this pattern. [2]

Question 1P

The diagram shows a circuit for taking measurements of the current in a lamp filament and the voltage across it.

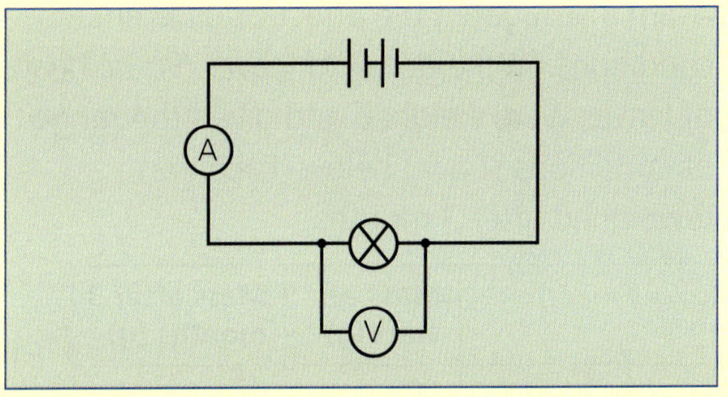

a i What component is connected in parallel with the lamp? [1]

ii What two components are connected in series with the lamp? [1]

iii What additional component could be used to vary the current in the circuit? [1]

b The graph on the next page shows how the resistance of the filament depends on the current passing in it.

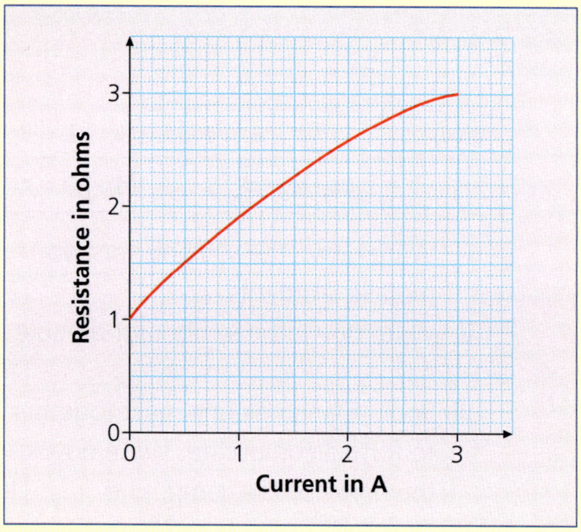

i Describe how the resistance changes as the current increases. [2]

ii What is the resistance of the filament when the current in it is 2.5 A? [1]

iii Calculate the voltage across the filament when the current is 2.5 A. [3]

Question 2B

Asam investigated the effect of different conditions on the decay of leaves. Equal heaps of leaves were weighed and given the range of conditions shown below. Each was reweighed after 3 months.

	Mass at start (g)	Mass after 3 months (g)
Cold and wet	100	79
Cold and dry	100	92
Warm and wet	100	62
Warm and dry	100	80

a Which conditions were best for the decay of leaves? [1]

b i How did Asam make sure that the investigation was a fair test? [2]

ii Suggest one other way in which Asam could make sure that the investigation was fair. [1]

c i During decay the leaves increased in temperature. How could Asam measure the temperature of the heaps of leaves accurately? [2]

ii Why did the temperature increase? [2]

d At the end of the investigation Asam put the decayed leaves on some plants. Explain why he did this. [2]

Question 2C

This question is about the Earth's atmosphere. The composition of the atmosphere is kept constant because some processes use up oxygen (respiration and combustion) and others produce oxygen (photosynthesis).

a Write down the name of the gas present in the Earth's atmosphere today in the largest amounts. [1]

b According to a recent magazine article, 300 years ago the atmosphere contained 38% oxygen. Today it contains about 20%. Explain why this change may have taken place. [4]

c Explain how the content of carbon dioxide has changed in the same period. [2]

Question 2P

The diagram shows the horizontal forces acting on a car.

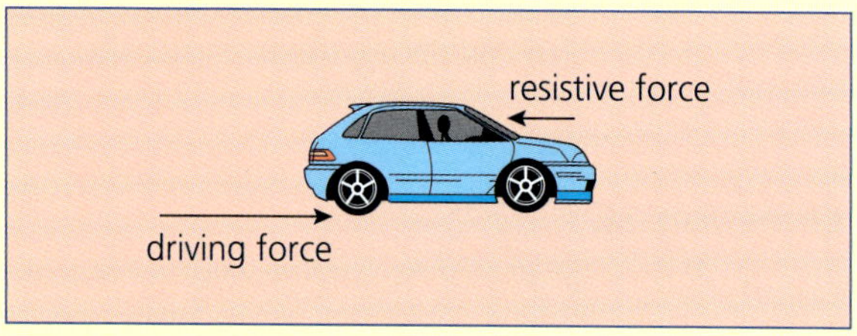

a Explain how you can tell from the diagram that the car is accelerating in a forward direction. [2]

b The car increases its speed from 5 m/s to 15 m/s in 4.0 s. Calculate the acceleration of the car. [3]

c How does the increased speed of the car affect:

  i The driver's reaction time? [1]

  ii The thinking distance when the driver sees a hazard? [1]

  iii The braking distance when the driver applies the brakes? [1]

Question 3B

The diagram below shows a healthy artery and a diseased artery. An unsuitable diet has resulted in the condition (arteriosclerosis).

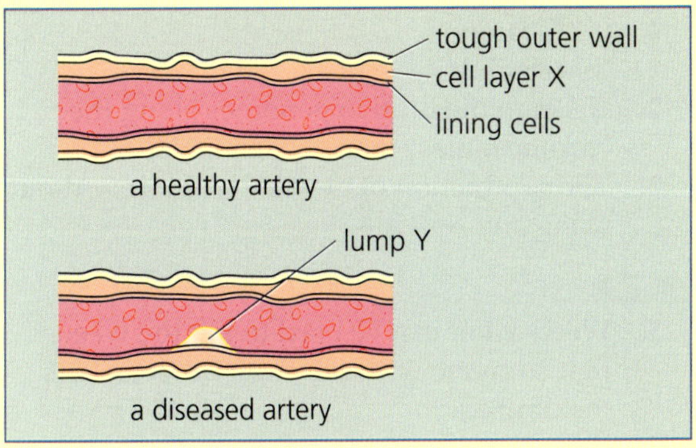

a Name cell layer X. [1]

b i What is lump Y? [1]

  ii Suggest a chemical in the diet that causes this condition. [1]

  iii What effect would the lump Y have on blood pressure in the artery? [1] blood flow through the artery? [1]

  iv If the lump continued to grow, how could this affect the heart? Give a reason for your answer. [2]

  v Suggest two ways that the above problem could be avoided. [2]

Question 3C

There are two lists below. One list is a list of alkali metals and the other is a list of halogens.

Alkali metals	**Halogens**
lithium	fluorine
sodium	chlorine
potassium	iodine

a Sodium reacts with chlorine to form sodium chloride, NaCl. Write down the name and formula of the compound of potassium and iodine. [2]

b Which alkali metal and which halogen react together most vigorously? Explain your choices.

c Electrolysis of molten sodium chloride produces two products. What are the two products and at which electrode is each product formed? [2]

d Electrolysis of a concentrated solution of sodium chloride produces three useful products. Write down the three products and a use of each product. [6]

Answers to these questions can be found on page 145

Answers to end of spread questions

Module 1

END OF SPREAD QUESTIONS

P3

1. Suitable temperature and pH.
2. It is denatured or destroyed (NOT killed!)
3. The reaction is slower and enzyme eventually becomes inactive.
4. Nothing happens to protein in the mouth – there is no protease enzyme present.
5. The small intestine is very long, so has a large surface area. There are large numbers of villi and each has many microvilli.

P5

1. Some white blood cells can engulf microbes. Some can produce antibodies.
2. To prevent microbes from entering the bloodstream. They stop the person bleeding to death.
3. Too much light entering the eye can damage the retina. Too little light and you cannot see.
4. A sedative. Cirrhosis (hardening of the liver) or brain damage.

P7

1. Homeostasis is the way in which the body balances various processes to keep a constant internal environment.
2. The liver.
3. The kidneys.
4. The ureter.

P9

1. No nucleus, giving a greater surface area to take up oxygen. Also has haemoglobin to attract oxygen.
2. Sweat is produced by sweat gland, passes to skin surface, evaporates into air, evaporation fuelled by temperature.

PRACTICE MODULE TEST

1. D	6. B	11. A	16. C
2. D	7. B	12. B	17. C
3. B	8. B	13. B	18. A
4. B	9. A	14. A	19. B
5. C	10. B	15. C	20. B

Module 2

END OF SPREAD QUESTIONS

P15

1. (a) Oestrogen stimulates the build-up of the lining of the uterus wall.
   (b) Progesterone maintains the lining of the uterus.
2. Fertilisation is the fusion of a sperm with an egg cell.

P17

1. (a) Guanine,
   (b) adenine.
2. To map the human genomes along the chromosomes/map human DNA.
3. The production of new individuals without using any sex cells.

P19

1. Weed-killer can be used to kill the weeds that compete with the crop. Crop yield is maximised.
2. Plant growth.
3. Water, minerals.
4. Fossils exist, which show changes through time.
5. The others die out (selected against).

P20

1. GM soya beans have received a gene from another species to become resistant.
2. They have a high yield because weed-killer kills weeds, which compete for water/minerals. Crop gets more nutrients.

P21

1. Sulphur dioxide mixes with water in clouds, clouds are blown to Sweden, acid rain produced, pollutes the country.
2. Sulphur dioxide, carbon monoxide and nitrogen oxides and (excess) cargon dioxide.

PRACTICE MODULE TEST

1. B	6. C	11. C	16. B
2. A	7. A	12. C	17. D
3. D	8. B	13. C	18. B
4. C	9. B	14. B	19. B
5. A	10. D	15. A	20. C

Module 3

END OF SPREAD QUESTIONS

P27

1. Phosphorus.
2. Non-metal.
3. Potassium.
4. Seven.

P28

1. Protons and neutrons.
2. Electron.
3. Electron.

P31

1. Catalyst.
2. Shorter.
3. Enzyme.
4. It has a smaller particle size, so more surface area to react.

P33

1. Fluorine.
2. Potassium chloride and bromine.
3. Displacement.
4. Chlorine.

PRACTICE MODULE TEST

1.	D	**6.**	B	**11.**	C	**16.**	C
2.	C	**7.**	A	**12.**	D	**17.**	C
3.	B	**8.**	C	**13.**	C	**18.**	B
4.	C	**9.**	D	**14.**	A	**19.**	A
5.	A	**10.**	A	**15.**	C	**20.**	D

Module 4

END OF SPREAD QUESTIONS

P39

1. Hydrogen and carbon.
2. Fractional distillation.
3. High temperatures, high pressure and the absence of oxygen.
4. Near the top.

P40

1. Methane.
2. Carbon dioxide and water.
3. Carbon monoxide.

P41

1. Alkanes
2. Ten.

P42

1. Carbon dioxide.
2. Cheese and yoghurt.

P43

1. Sulphuric acid.
2. As a fertiliser.

PRACTICE MODULE TEST

1.	A	**6.**	C	**11.**	C	**16.**	B
2.	C	**7.**	C	**12.**	B	**17.**	C
3.	B	**8.**	D	**13.**	A	**18.**	A
4.	A	**9.**	D	**14.**	D	**19.**	B
5.	A	**10.**	D	**15.**	C	**20.**	B

Module 5

END OF SPREAD QUESTIONS

P49

1. Direct current passes in the same direction all the time. Alternating current changes direction.
2. In parallel.
3. 10.0 V.
4. A light-dependent resistor (LDR).

P51

1. The live conductor.
2. The earth.
3. It melts.

P53

1. They rotate inside copper coils.
2. Transformers.
3. Fossil fuels.
4. Cavity wall insulation.

PRACTICE MODULE TEST

1.	D	**6.**	B	**11.**	B	**16.**	D
2.	A	**7.**	B	**12.**	C	**17.**	D
3.	A	**8.**	C	**13.**	B	**18.**	A
4.	D	**9.**	D	**14.**	D	**19.**	B
5.	B	**10.**	C	**15.**	C	**20.**	B

Module 6

END OF SPREAD QUESTIONS

P59

1. Radio waves.
2. Its speed changes.
3. 630 m.
4. Ultrasound has a higher frequency or cannot be heard by humans.

P61

1. Gravitational forces causing part of the dust cloud to collapse.
2. Jupiter is very massive.
3 They can be in any direction and they are elliptical.

P63

1. Eight protons and seven neutrons.
2. They have the same number of protons and different numbers of neutrons.
3. The alpha radiation cannot penetrate the casing of the smoke alarm.

PRACTICE MODULE TEST

1. D	7. D	13. D	19. C
2. D	8. C	14. A	20. D
3. C	9. B	15. A	21. C
4. A	10. B	16. C	22. B
5. D	11. B	17. D	23. A
6. A	12. C	18. B	24. C

Module 7

END OF SPREAD QUESTIONS

P69

1. (a) Xylem, (b) phloem.
2. The movement of water molecules through a selectively permeable membrane from a solution of lower concentration to a solution of higher concentration.
3. Guard cells.

P71

1. Producers or green plants.
2. Through respiration and through excretion.
3. Biodiversity is reduced.
4. Weeds reduce the amount of wheat produced because the weeds compete for light, water and minerals.

P73

1. Suitable temperature, suitable pH, oxygen or air.
2. To recycle useful materials, to reduce organic waste.
3. To add air or oxygen for microbe respiration.
4. Respiration, photosynthesis, combustion.
5. Use of wood for building or furniture. To use the land for human activities such as keeping animals or building factories.
6. Where microorganisms use atmospheric nitrogen to make nitrogen compounds.

P75

1. Pesticides kill the organisms that attack the crop plants.
2. Selective herbicide kills weeds, so the crop grows better.
3. Organic.
4. Biological control/predators.

PRACTICE MODULE TEST

1. D	6. C	11. B	16. A
2. C	7. C	12. A	17. A
3. D	8. B	13. B	18. C
4. A	9. C	14. C	19. C
5. A	10. B	15. B	20. A

Module 8

END OF SPREAD QUESTIONS

P81

1. It contracts, causing a fall in the pressure inside the lungs.
2. The alveoli provide a high surface area for oxygen to pass into the blood, and carbon dioxide to pass out of the lungs.
3. (1) The air is warmed (less of a shock to the lungs). (2) Dust and microbes are filtered out of the air before it enters the lungs.

P83

1. The valve makes sure that blood does not go back from the ventricle into the atrium and makes sure that blood passes out of the heart.
2. The left and right ventricles.
3. It contracts, helping to push blood along the artery.

P85

1. Oxygen, water.
2. In thc cytoplasm plus mitochondria.
3. Aerobic respiration.

P87

1. An aerosol is used in the lungs, to insert "healthy" genes.
2. The haemoglobin of sickled red blood cells is less efficient than normal haemoglobin – so less oxygen is transported.
3. The red cells jam together and cause a blockage.

PRACTICE MODULE TEST

1. A	6. A	11. B	16. A
2. C	7. D	12. A	17. B
3. B	8. A	13. C	18. C
4. D	9. D	14. C	19. B
5. A	10. B	15. D	20. B

Module 9

END OF SPREAD QUESTIONS

P93

1. Sodium
2. Iron ore, coke, limestone
3. Reduction
4. Deposited on the cathode

P94

1. C
2. A

P95

1. Sodium hydroxide
2. Lithium hydroxide + hydrogen
   Potassium hydroxide + hydrogen
3. More reactive

P97

1. Limestone
2. Marble
3. Granite
4. Igneous

P99

1. Nitrogen
2. Oxygen
3. Produces carbon dioxide
4. Nitrogen and hydrogen
5. Helium

PRACTICE MODULE TEST

1.	C	**6.**	C	**11.**	A	**16.**	B
2.	D	**7.**	D	**12.**	D	**17.**	A
3.	A	**8.**	D	**13.**	D	**18.**	B
4.	A	**9.**	C	**14.**	C	**19.**	B
5.	A	**10.**	B	**15.**	A	**20.**	D

Module 10

END OF SPREAD QUESTIONS

P105

1. 15
2. 15
3. 16
4. 8
5. oxygen – 16 8
   oxygen – 18 10

P108

1. **a** ionic
   b covalent
2. ionic
3. covalent
4. true

P109

1. + energy on left hand side
2. endothermic
3. exothermic
4. 12
5. 2
6. 44
7. 17

PRACTICE MODULE TEST

1.	B	**6.**	C	**11.**	C	**16.**	B
2.	D	**7.**	C	**12.**	C	**17.**	D
3.	B	**8.**	A	**13.**	C	**18.**	A
4.	A	**9.**	B	**14.**	D	**19.**	A
5.	D	**10.**	C	**15.**	B	**20.**	B

Module 11

END OF SPREAD QUESTIONS

P116

1. A distance a vehicle travels during the driver's reaction time.
2. Terminal velocity.
3. 1.25 m/s^2.

P117

1. Gravitational potential energy.
2. 4500 J.
3. Kinetic energy to gravitational potential energy.

P119

1. Seismic waves.
2. It melts in the magma.
3. Continental plates moving away from each other.

P121

1. It decreases.
2. (a) 600 Bq. (b) 300 Bq.
3. Cloth and wood.

PRACTICE MODULE TEST

1.	D	**7.**	A	**13.**	D	**19.**	D
2.	B	**8.**	C	**14.**	C	**20.**	A
3.	B	**9.**	A	**15.**	B	**21.**	C
4.	D	**10.**	C	**16.**	D	**22.**	D
5.	B	**11.**	A	**17.**	B	**23.**	C
6.	C	**12.**	D	**18.**	D	**24.**	A

Module 12

END OF SPREAD QUESTIONS

P127

1. Electrostatic and repulsive.
2. **a** negative **b** positive
3. It provides a rate for charge to pass to the ground.

P129

1. The size of a current in A is equal to the rate of flow of charge in C/s.
2. 2280 W.
3. To minimise the current, reducing the power losses.

P131

1. 1300 m/s.
2. The angle of incidence is greater than the critical angle.
3. The gap is many wavelengths wide for light but less than a wavelength for sound.

P133

1. (a) 2.5 cm. (b) That a force of 20 N does not stretch the spring beyond the linear part of the extension–force graph.
2. By the particles colliding with the container walls.

PRACTICE MODULE TEST

1.	D	**7.**	D	**13.**	C	**19.**	D
2.	C	**8.**	D	**14.**	A	**20.**	D
3.	D	**9.**	A	**15.**	B	**21.**	C
4.	A	**10.**	B	**16.**	D	**22.**	B
5.	D	**11.**	D	**17.**	C	**23.**	D
6.	A	**12.**	D	**18.**	B	**24.**	A

Answers to exam questions

Question 1B

a *Sweat pore.*

b i *Urea, water, sweat (any two).*
  ii *Through the blood/through capillaries.*
  iii *Sweat lies on skin, evaporation takes place, heat energy from body needed (for evaporation to take place), so body cools down (any three).*

c *Body temperature increases.*

d *Skin cells are tough/have keratin; form a barrier; sedum/oil produced; contains a chemical that kills bacteria/contains lysozyme (any three).*

Question 1C

a *Protons and neutrons (both required).*

b i *Na, Mg, Al (any two).*
  ii *Ar*
  iii *Sodium chloride.*
  iv *15*
  v *From left to right, each element has one more electron than the previous one (or words to that effect) OR The number of outer electrons is the same as the group number.*

Question 1P

a i *Voltmeter*
  ii *Ammeter and battery.*
  iii *Variable resistor.*

b i *The resistance increases in a non-linear way/not in proportion.*
  ii *2.8 Ω*
  ii *Voltage = current x resistance (or symbols)*
    = 2.5 A x 2.8 Ω
    = 7.0 V
  (one mark for each line)

Question 2B

a *Warm and wet.*

b i *He used equal amounts of leaves and left them for the same time.*
  ii *By using the same type of leaves.*

c i *Use a thermometer; use temperature probe + computer or datalogger; repeat and take average.*
  ii *Respiration (of bacteria).*

d *The decayed leaves are a fertiliser; increase plant growth; reduce water loss; nitrate supplied (any two).*

Question 2C

a *Nitrogen.*

b *Increased population; more respiration/produce more carbon dioxide; much greater use of (fossil) fuels/coal; uses up oxygen and produces carbon dioxide; increased pollution; kills algae/plants so reducing photosynthesis/less oxygen released/ destruction of forests/more buildings (one mark each for any three points, plus one mark for answer written in sentences with correct punctuation and grammar).*

c *More carbon dioxide; decreasing oxygen is linked to increasing carbon dioxide.*

Question 2P

a *The driving force is greater than the resistive force; so there is an unbalanced force in the forward direction.*

b *Acceleration = increase in velocity ÷ time taken (or symbols)*
  = 10 m/s ÷ 4.0 s
  = 2.5 m/s^2
  (one mark for each line)

c i *No effect.*
  ii *Increases.*
  iii *Increases.*

Question 3B

a *Muscle.*

b i *Fat/atheroma/cholesterol build-up.*
  ii *Animal fat/saturated fat.*
  iii *Increase.*
  Slow it down.
  iv *Heart attack, caused by lack of oxygen or glucose to the heart.*
  v *More exercise to use up fat in diet; eat less fat.*

Question 3C

a *potassium iodide*
  KI

b *Potassium and fluorine*
  Most reactive halogen and most reactive alkali metal

c *Sodium at the cathode*
  Chlorine at the anode

d

Sodium hydroxide	*soap making*
Hydrogen	*making ammonia or margarine*
Chlorine	*killing bacteria in water*

Getting the grade you deserve

Exams are an opportunity for you to show just how much you have learnt in all your science lessons. It would be a great shame if you didn't get all the marks you deserve.

Knowing what to expect in the exam will help you make the most of your scientific skills and knowledge. The advice on these pages will help you to understand what the examiner is asking you to do and help you to prepare in the best way possible.

What types of questions will I have to answer?

You will find a number of different types of questions in each exam paper. These include:

- sentence completion – you may or may not be given the responses to choose from;
- short-answer questions – these can be answered with a single word or phrase or by linking boxes;
- data handling questions – these give you information, usually in the form of a table or a graph, that you have to use to answer the question;
- long-answer questions – these need you to make at least two points in one or more sentences and are worth at least two marks;
- calculations – you need to recall or select the correct relationship and use it correctly to calculate the size of a quantity.

How should I start to answer a question?

Many questions begin with a short piece of introductory material that gives you some information about a scientific context and may include a diagram. This introduction often contains key information that you need to answer the question.

Many candidates do not bother to read the introduction to a question. They go straight to the questions being asked and then find that they do not know the answers. The answers may be staring you in the face!

- Read the introduction carefully. If it's lengthy read it two or three times.
- Underline key points.

- Examiners go to great lengths to put the least number of words possible in a question. They only put things in that are important.
- When you have put together an answer in your head, refer back to the introductory material before putting pen to paper.

How can I gain the most marks?

First, always look at how many marks are allocated to the answer. This is printed in brackets after the answer space.

- If there are two marks then you need to make *two* separate correct points to gain them both.
- If there is only one mark and you give two answers, one of which is correct and one of which is wrong, you will not be awarded any marks for your answer.

Then, look at the cue word that the question begins with. The most common cue words are: **State** or **give** or **name**

A single word, phrase or sentence is needed.

Describe

This requires a description of:

- a scientific process;
- how one variable is related to another;
- a trend or pattern in data – this will be given either in a table or on a graph

Explain

This is asking you to give reasons to support your answer. A simple description is likely to gain only one mark out of a possible three. Your answer should include "because" followed by the reasons. Check carefully to see if you really have "explained".

Suggest

Suggest can be asking for a description but **suggest why** is usually asking for an explanation. Suggest is used instead of describe or explain for a number of reasons:

- the question might involve an application of science that you are not required to be familiar with;
- there might be no clear correct answer;
- the question might ask you to make a prediction.

Whatever the case, you are expected to use your knowledge and understanding of science to answer the question.

How should I approach calculations?

Calculations should always be set out in a clear, logical order. There may be a "quality of written communication" mark just for doing this. The steps to take are:

- Write down the relationship that you are using in either words or standard symbols, whether it is one you need to recall or one that is given on the exam paper.
- Write out the relationship with the correct quantities written in the place of the words or symbols.
- Calculate the final answer and state the correct units.

One mark out of the 30 on each exam paper requires knowledge of a correct scientific unit.

How are the marks awarded for drawing a graph?

You will be given a grid that already has the scales and the axes labelled. Three marks are available.

- two marks for plotting the points correctly;
- one mark for drawing the best-fit straight line or smooth curve.

Points to note when drawing graphs are:

- use a pencil so that you can erase mistakes;
- make each plotted point clearly visible – dots are easily hidden behind a line, so use crosses;
- never draw a line by joining the plotted points together, use a smooth curve or line of best fit;
- never draw a line by joining the first and last points together – there is no reason why these should be any more reliable than the others;
- use a transparent ruler to draw a straight line, and judge it so that there are as many points above the line as there are below it;
- check any points that seem to be a long way from the line – you may have made a mistake.

Preparing for exams

Is revision really important?

Effective revision is important because it:

- reminds you of key facts that you have learned throughout the course or module;
- brings together similar concepts and ideas from different modules;
- gives you confidence that you are well prepared for a module test or terminal exam.

What's the best way to revise?

Not by reading through this or any other revision book! In using this book:

- you should work your way through the text, using a notebook to jot down key facts and ideas;
- refer to a textbook to clarify any points that you are unsure about;
- think about and answer all the questions – check your answers with those given in the text and make sure that you understand how your own answers can be improved;
- refer back to your notebook and condense what you have already written.

In using other sources:

- choose sources that give you practice in answering exam questions;
- you can order copies of past papers from Edexcel's website;
- remember that questions are not usually repeated from year to year, so simply rehearsing answers to the previous year's examination is not likely to be very effective preparation.

How should I organise my revision programme?

The best advice is:

- start well ahead, so that you are not under pressure for time;
- write out a revision timetable and stick to it;
- on the night before an important module test or exam, give your brain a rest – too much cramming leads to confusion.

Assessing ideas and evidence

What's it worth?

The assessment of ideas and evidence in science has to be worth 5% of all the available marks. However, coursework and module tests do not examine this, so all of the assessment is done on the final exam papers. This means that 10% of the marks on each paper, or three marks out of 30, are devoted to assessing this aspect of your course.

What are the examiners looking for?

There are four aspects of ideas and evidence in science that will be examined:

1. How scientific ideas are presented, evaluated and disseminated.

   This is straightforward. Questions will ask you how scientists communicate with other scientists and make their ideas known throughout the world. The answers are through international conferences, and writing in books and magazines such as *Nature*, *Scientific American* and *New Scientist*.

2. How scientific controversies can arise from different ways of interpreting empirical evidence.

   The phrase "empirical evidence" means evidence gathered from experiments or data collection. Questions that assess this aspect of ideas and evidence are likely to be about situations where the scientific evidence is unclear – for example the evidence linking electricity power lines or nuclear power stations to cancer. You should be prepared to give balanced arguments, emphasising the different ways in which the evidence can be judged.

3. Ways in which scientific work may be affected by the context in which it takes place

   A good example of this is the cloning of animals and the possibility of cloning humans. You will not be expected to know all the details of "Dolly the sheep", as these will be given to you in the question. You will be expected to give the arguments about whether human cloning should be allowed, or whether human fetuses should be developed just to obtain important biochemicals from them.

4. Ways to consider the power and limitations of science in addressing industrial, social and environmental questions, including the kinds of questions science can and cannot answer, uncertainties in scientific knowledge and the ethical issues involved.

   There are lots of topical issues and examples in recent history of questions that science cannot answer or has got the answers wrong. Examples include the BSE and foot and mouth crises. You need to be able to give reasons as to why science can or cannot provide the answers to these. The reasons may be that scientists are often unable to experiment on humans or do not have enough evidence to predict the effects of action or inaction.

How will I know which questions assess ideas and evidence?

Unlike the assessment of written communication, there will not be an icon on exam papers to show where ideas and evidence is being assessed. Sometimes it will be clear, for example "How do scientists communicate their findings to other scientists?" At other times it will not be so clear.

The questions assessing ideas and evidence will always be embodied within other questions. Remember, keep an open mind, be prepared to make suggestions and put together a logical argument from both points of view when answering questions about issues where there is no definitive answer.

1	2											3	4	5	6	7	0 (or 8)
H 1 hydrogen																	He 2 helium
Li 3 lithium	Be 4 berylium											B 5 boron	C 6 carbon	N 7 nitrogen	O 8 oxygen	F 9 fluorine	Ne 10 neon
Na 11 sodium	Mg 12 magnesium											Al 13 aluminium	Si 14 silicon	P 15 phosphorous	S 16 sulphur	Cl 17 chlorine	Ar 18 argon
K 19 potassium	Ca 20 calcium	Sc 21 scandium	Ti 22 titanium	V 23 vanadium	Cr 24 chromium	Mn 25 manganese	Fe 26 iron	Co 27 cobalt	Ni 28 nickel	Cu 29 copper	Zn 30 zinc	Ga 31 gallium	Ge 32 germanium	As 33 arsenic	Se 34 selenium	Br 35 bromine	Kr 36 krypton
Rb 37 rubidium	Sr 38 strontium	Y 39 yttrium	Zr 40 zirconium	Nb 41 niobium	Mo 42 molybdenum	Tc 43 technetium	Ru 44 ruthenium	Rh 45 rhodium	Pd 46 palladium	Ag 47 silver	Cd 48 cadmium	In 49 indium	Sn 50 tin	Sb 51 antimony	Te 52 tellurium	I 53 iodine	Xe 54 xenon
Cs 55 caesium	Ba 56 barium	La 57 lanthanum	Hf 72 hafnium	Ta 73 tantalum	W 74 tungsten	Re 75 rhenium	Os 76 osmium	Ir 77 iridium	Pt 78 platinum	Au 79 gold	Hg 80 mercury	Ti 81 thallium	Pb 82 lead	Bi 83 bismuth	Po 84 polonium	At 85 astatine	Rn 86 radon

group numbers

= metals

= non-metals

= semi-metal

metals

non-metals

Index

L

M

N

O

P

R